China Tripping

悟 *(wù)* means *"to realize, comprehend, come clear about"* and is perhaps the best single-character approximation of the idea of *"Aha!"* that runs through this book.

China Tripping

Encountering the Everyday in the People's Republic

Edited by
Jeremy A. Murray, Perry Link,
and Paul G. Pickowicz

ROWMAN & LITTLEFIELD
Lanham • Boulder • New York • London

Published by Rowman & Littlefield
An imprint of The Rowman & Littlefield Publishing Group, Inc.
4501 Forbes Boulevard, Suite 200, Lanham, Maryland 20706
www.rowman.com

6 Tinworth Street, London SE11 5AL, United Kingdom

British Library Cataloguing in Publication Information Available

Library of Congress Cataloging-in-Publication Data

Names: Murray, Jeremy A., editor. | Link, E. Perry (Eugene Perry), 1944– editor. | Pickowicz, Paul, editor.
Title: China tripping : encountering the everyday in the People's Republic / edited by Jeremy A. Murray, Perry Link, and Paul G. Pickowicz.
Description: Lanham : Rowman & Littlefield, [2019]
Identifiers: LCCN 2018042107 (print) | LCCN 2018050722 (ebook) | ISBN 9781538123713 (electronic) | ISBN 9781538123690 (cloth : alk. paper) | ISBN 9781538123706 (pbk. : alk. paper)
Subjects: LCSH: China—Description and travel. | Americans—China—20th century. | Americans—China—21st century. | China—Social life and customs—1976–2002. | China—Social life and customs—2002–
Classification: LCC DS712 (ebook) | LCC DS712 .C48215 2019 (print) | DDC 951.05—dc23
LC record available at https://lccn.loc.gov/2018042107

Printed in the United States of America

Contents

Acknowledgments

Planning for *China Tripping* began as a series of meetings held at California State University, San Bernardino, and in Riverside and La Jolla, California. The editors wish to thank the following people and units at CSUSB for their generous support before, during, and after these gatherings: History Department chair Tiffany Jones, History Department coordinator Pamela Crosson, the CSUSB History Club/ Phi Alpha Theta, and the staff of Pfau Library. We are also grateful for support from the Chancellorial Chair for Teaching Across Disciplines at the University of California, Riverside, and the Endowed Chair in Modern Chinese History at the University of California, San Diego.

The two reflections written by Professor Charlotte Furth (part III) are borrowed, with thanks, from her book *Opening to China: A Memoir of Normalization, 1981–82* (Amherst, NY: Cambria Press, 2017), pp. 29–31 and 37–39. Some material by Jeffrey Wasserstrom (part V) first appeared in "Chinese Hits Unknown in the West," a commentary by the author that appeared on the website of the *Times Literary Supplement* (London) on October 26, 2016.

Special thanks to Li Huai of the UC San Diego Visual Arts Department for contributing both the striking calligraphy of 悟 (wù) and the splendid image that graces the cover of this book and so nicely captures the sense of adventure associated with "China tripping." Thanks to our production editor, Jehanne Schweitzer, and the superb staff at

Rowman & Littlefield. Finally, we are delighted to acknowledge the tireless work of our editor, Susan McEachern. Our multiyear relationship with Susan continues to grow in many wonderful directions.

Jeremy A. Murray
Perry Link
Paul G. Pickowicz

Introduction

From the middle of the nineteenth century to the middle of the twentieth century, American China experts, including scholars, journalists, and expatriates, traveled back and forth to China all the time for short and long stays. No big deal. Their professions involved researching China and understanding China whether the topic was the ancient past or the complicated present. In both theory and practice, this type of knowledge acquisition could be gained outside China. But it was natural and sensible and desirable to do as much of it as possible while residing or traveling in China itself. These people were often called "Old China Hands" or *Zhongguo tong* (中國通), that is, foreigners who possessed impressive knowledge of China. Students of Britain want to spend time in Britain. Egypt specialists want to spend time in Egypt. China hands want to spend time in China. There's nothing strange about it.

But the situation for American and nearly all foreign China specialists changed rather abruptly following the civil war victory of the Communist Party in 1949. Owing to fierce global Cold War antagonisms, as well as rapidly evolving post-revolution domestic political eruptions, China became increasingly isolated from the international community in the 1950s and 1960s. The United States and China had no diplomatic relations and even went to war in Korea in the early 1950s. This generated intense speculation about what was really going on behind the "Bamboo Curtain."

1

Scholarly and journalistic interest in China did not decline after direct access to China became virtually impossible for Americans who considered themselves professional China experts. On the contrary, their interest steadily intensified. In the 1950s and 1960s, many young Americans dedicated themselves to the study of China's past and present without any real hope of setting foot in China. This was frustrating. But the passion was always there. Whether the main research interest was the pre-Communist period or the new People's Republic, there was a very human and burning desire to travel, reside, and do research in China. Nonetheless, China remained remarkably isolated. For more than two decades after 1949, its leaders seemed inward looking, and its citizens were urged and pressured to be suspicious of outsiders. Not surprisingly, this isolation served to stimulate the desire of China specialists throughout the world to experience the country firsthand. And not surprisingly, many in China were in fact intensely curious about the outside world.

Thanks to tangled geopolitical shifts that began unfolding in the very early 1970s, the situation began to change. China fought a brief border war in 1969 with the Soviet Union, its onetime Cold War ally. It was risky, but it made sense for China's leaders to think about significantly better relations with the United States and other former adversaries. China was diplomatically isolated and dangerously stagnant. American policy makers, for their part, began to take seriously the idea of meaningful relations with China, in part as a way of putting pressure on the Soviet Union.

As a consequence of this wheeling and dealing, the door opened a bit, and American access to China was initiated when an American table-tennis team, competing in Japan, received a surprise invitation to visit China in April 1971. Very slowly, but ever so surely, China's isolation began to give way as Americans and other foreigners, including China experts, jumped at the chance to engage in "China tripping."

China tripping involved and still involves brief, longer, and even extended stays in China for American and other foreign passport holders. As self-respecting professionals, scholarly and journalistic China trippers wrote up and published their formal research about the past and present. These writings were widely read and increasingly influential. But China tripping—then and now—involved much more than the professional side of doing one's job. Whether it was one's first, third, tenth, or twenty-fifth trip, new China hands encountered many unscripted and unexpected things in daily life as they wandered around China and interacted with official "minders" as well as ordinary citizens. When trippers met each other, they often traded stories that began with, "Guess what happened to me the other day!"

In short, China tripping involved a fascinating array of human encounters. Many of these encounters were startling precisely because China had been so isolated for so long, and foreign trippers—including China experts—had very little knowledge of daily life in a place as large and immensely diverse as China. And the people they encountered in China had relatively little understanding of the complexities of life outside China. Stereotypes and simplistic assumptions abounded on all sides.

We like the "China tripping" concept for various reasons, but mainly because it has many different levels of meaning. At the most obvious level it means, "I recently went on a trip to China." But it can also mean, "I was in China and I was constantly tripping over things that I hadn't seen before or expected." This kind of tripping or stumbling can be a function of ignorance or deeply rooted misconceptions. It could be funny, enlightening, and puzzling, even when it had nothing to do with one's formal work or research activity.

And, of course, China "tripping" can also involve getting high or stoned on China. Whether it was the miracles of herbal medicine, unfamiliar and "exotic" foods and beverages, or the allure of utopian revolutionary projects that one hoped could really address human sufferings, it was easy enough to "trip out" on a visit to China, though such highs could lead to hangovers.

Our book is different because it does not pay attention to the formal publications of academic and journalistic China trippers. Instead, it explores what a large group of known China specialists experienced in their daily lives while in China. The book is about China and its stunning people, but it is also about the China trippers themselves in the nearly fifty years since the surprise opening of 1971. Under what circumstances did the authors experience an "Aha!" moment? What do these moments tell us about China and its many types of people? What do the moments tell us about the trippers?

Instead of looking for formal and lengthy autobiographies and memoirs, we looked for very short, in-and-out vignettes and reflections. What follows are adventures of discovery and self-discovery. Some accounts are charming, some are funny, some are sad. Stereotypes of all sorts dissolve. Deep human friendships are made. Meanwhile, China itself is seen changing and evolving at breakneck pace. Its leaders decided it was necessary to "reform and open up," but from the perspective of the Party-state, how much openness is enough? At what point is global knowledge and contact perceived as a threat? What if ordinary citizens desire more openness than their leaders want? For their part, China trippers encountered, and still encounter, the very familiar as well as the brand-new and previously unimaginable every time they go to China. The learning process is open-ended as one meets new people and encounters unexpected phenomena.

The recollections included here cover a range of positive, negative, and ambiguous episodes. A traveler's most formative experiences in any country or culture may seem at first to be challenging or unsettling. But our intention here is not to portray China as exotic or treacherous. We authors have dedicated much of our lives to the study of China and the cultural bridge-building efforts that became our classroom lectures and our published writings. Furthermore, if there is indeed a common theme in this collection, perhaps it is that of the authors' wonder and discovery, and also, by implication, the theme of the authors' ignorance that preceded that new experience and understanding.

Our group of trippers is diverse. It includes women and men, various disciplinary researchers, people from differing ethnic backgrounds, as well as older, middle-aged, and younger trippers. Our trippers have tried very hard not to be preachy or hit the reader over the head with the only possible "meaning" of their vignettes. We believe that each reflection contains various "takeaways" for readers, but you the reader can decide for yourself what the takeaways are. Over the decades, whenever China trippers met, they told lively stories about things they experienced during their latest adventures, but they rarely, if ever, wrote up their random personal encounters.

So let us now consider what our China trippers, gathered for the purposes of this book, have to say. Let us befriend a street hawker, discover a home disco, mingle with devout Roman Catholics, meet long-lost relatives, interact with a psychic, ride on horseback with Tibetans, immerse ourselves in the bustling flea market scene, listen to a dear friend describe the pain of domestic violence, unravel the politics of stamp collecting, and consider the unexpected impact of Mickey Mouse. And more.

Part I

悟

Early Trippers

Very few Westerners lived in China from the early 1950s until the late 1970s. A few Western embassies did have modest staffs, and a group of Western sympathizers made up a small community in Beijing. But there was not much back-and-forth between either of these groups and the ocean of interested people on the outside. For young Western China scholars—as well as journalists, business people, and others—no destination on earth was more intriguing or alluring than the People's Republic of China (PRC). Few got there, and in order to have a chance, it helped to be "friendly" to the socialist system. Some of our authors were active in a group called the Committee of Concerned Asian Scholars (CCAS)—mostly Americans, and mostly graduate students—who had come together in opposition to the United States' war in Vietnam. They had no firsthand knowledge of the PRC, but hoped that it would resemble the ideals that its publications projected. Our authors also include members of the Committee on Scholarly Communication with the People's Republic of China (CSCPRC), a subcommittee of the U.S. National Academy of Sciences, which handled many of the early scholarly exchanges with China from the U.S. side.

悟

DIRTY UNDERWEAR

Paul G. Pickowicz

1971

It was midsummer 1971 and I was traveling through China with a group of American graduate students, most based in Hong Kong for a year of research on China. The group consisted of young, middle-class men and women whose passionate and self-righteous political views centered on staunch opposition to America's war in Vietnam. As students of China, we all had an intense curiosity about Mao's China and considered ourselves fortunate to be in the first group of U.S. China scholars since 1949 to get visas to visit China. China and the United States had no diplomatic relations. We thought of ourselves as goodwill ambassadors engaged in people's diplomacy.

Like most of the others, my college and early graduate school years coincided with the rise of the student, civil rights, peace, and counter-culture movements of the 1960s. It was not okay to behave like an elit-ist or to think you were better than others. At the rhetorical level, and often in practice, students espoused egalitarianism. Men and women are equal, people of all colors are equal, and people of all nations are equal. Stand proudly with the underdogs of this world.

Traveling through China that hot summer on a carefully scripted guided tour, we were exposed time and again to slogans and propa-ganda of the mid–Cultural Revolution period that emphasized some of the same themes. Don't act high and mighty. Live simply. Don't exploit others. Be one with the people. Our hosts were clearly reaching out with this message.

We were all eager to counter stereotypes and wanted our Chinese hosts to see that ordinary Americans were not warmongers and spoke the language of peace and equality. This dynamic gave rise to some not-so-subtle competition among group members who wanted to show that their idealistic talk was not just empty words. This meant doing virtuous things and taking notice when others knowingly or unknowingly exhibited self-centered behavior.

In my case, for instance, I made a decision at the outset to hand-wash all my dirty clothes—socks and underwear included. With no laundries available, this approach made political sense. It was a superb example of living simply. How could I ask hotel staff members to wash *my* underwear? What kind of a statement would that be? Instead, I would rely on myself.

But there were two serious problems. First, as a simple student, I did not have many clothes and ran out of clean ones very quickly. Second, everywhere I went in the first half of this tour of revolutionary China—Guangzhou, Shanghai, Suzhou, and Nanjing—was terribly hot and humid. I diligently hand-washed my dirty socks and underwear along the way, but nothing would dry out. None of the hotels were air-conditioned. So, after each stop, I packed up my wet (and by now smelly) clothes and moved on to the next place. By the time I reached the Xinqiao Hotel in Beijing, the situation was pretty bad.

In those days, it was often the case that hotels were completely empty: lots of staff, but no guests. Certainly, if there were other guests, they would be visible in the dining room. The Xinqiao Hotel seemed empty. I was in desperate need of clean, dry socks and underwear, so I set off one morning with a bag of my wet, stinking things. My room was on the second floor, so I decided to go quietly up to higher floors in search of hotel staff, hoping that none of my travel mates would see me.

The fourth floor was deserted. It looked like all the doors were shut. Certainly there were staff members somewhere. Suddenly at the end of one corridor, I noticed an open door! I knocked gently on the open door and slowly entered with my sack of stinking socks and underwear. There were five or six young women seated on the beds or standing, and all of them looked up at me as I entered. No one said anything. Feeling uncomfortable and awkward, I spoke sheepishly in Chinese.

"Excuse me. I'm very sorry to disturb you. I don't mean to bother you. I'm in room 216 and I'll just leave this bag of laundry here and be off. No rush. Take your time." I slipped away, quite proud of myself and not really wanting to deal with the issue of whether I was engaging in exploitative behavior. In any case, none of my travel mates had seen me.

We had another busy day of guided tours of model revolutionary units full of apparently exemplary, model citizens. Back at the hotel we were finishing dinner in the cavernous dining room that was always

empty, except for us. Then I noticed that one of our minders, a pleasant young woman named Li, was standing in the wings and waving
me over. As I approached her, I noticed that she was holding that very
same sack of stinking socks and underwear that I had handed over to
the staff on the fourth floor in the morning. "What is she doing holding my clean clothes?" I wondered. "What if my friends notice?" But
I could tell upon closer inspection that the unmentionables were not
clean. They were still very damp and very smelly.

Li asked politely, "Did you drop off this dirty laundry on the fourth
floor this morning?"

"Yes, I brought it up to the staff."

"Those women aren't staff," she said in hushed tones as she handed
me the foul bag. "They are a delegation of women revolutionary fighters from the South Vietnam National Liberation Front."

悟

CHINA WAS NOT UTOPIA

Anita Chan

1971

I grew up in the 1950s in Hong Kong in a lower-middle-class family
with very modestly educated, apolitical parents. I went to school at an
anti-Communist Catholic school that made little girls attend church,
was spoon-fed by an exam-oriented educational system that regarded
Hong Kong and Chinese history as having terminated in 1911, and, in
a course on Chinese geography at the University of Hong Kong, took
notes furiously on the exact whereabouts of Chinese mountains and
rivers to make sure I could regurgitate these facts at the three-hour
year-end examination. I never heard words like Marxism or commu-
nism in any of the classes I attended. I was a white sheet of paper on
which anything could have been written.

Like most Hong Kong students at that time, I barely read anything
that was not useful for passing exams. I did have a vague image of
China—it had to be a horrible place. People were dirt poor and were
ruled by a *gongchandang* (Communist Party) that made almost noth-

ing available to its people. I knew this as a child because when some relatives went to visit relatives across the border, they brought with them bundles of old clothes and light bulbs. How can people not have light bulbs!?

My father's twelve siblings were split into two groups—one group, like my father, remained in Hong Kong, and another group did not return to Hong Kong after fighting in China during the war with Japan. Many years later, I understood they were the ones with socialist inclinations who had wanted to work for the motherland, and that most of them ended up suffering for their idealistic patriotic choice. Because of their Hong Kong background, after the Cultural Revolution erupted in 1966 they were considered politically unreliable.

One of my aunts who had remained in Hong Kong, Fourth Aunt, liked going back and forth to keep in touch with her brothers and sisters in China, and from the 1950s onward, she came back telling everyone it was not so bad there. Her Hong Kong siblings did not believe her. I heard sly remarks about her liking the Communists. But except for when Fourth Aunt insisted on giving us news, our close relatives in China were not a subject of conversation in the extended family circle. My parents never communicated with any of them. I think my father's attitude was: it serves them right for staying behind after the War.

The image I had of China worsened in 1968 during the Cultural Revolution when bashed and decomposed bodies, sometimes tied up in pairs by ropes, floated down into Hong Kong waters from the West River. Seeing disturbing photos of them in newspapers. I could not stop worrying when I went swimming in Repulse Bay that I might bump against one of the corpses, and I had to keep reminding myself this was impossible because the beach is on the southern side of Hong Kong Island.

In 1970, I returned to Hong Kong after studying for a master's in geography at York University in Canada. I soon became acquainted with some American postgraduate students who were in Hong Kong to study China. Several of them were members of the Committee of Concerned Asian Scholars, which had been founded by opponents of America's involvement in the Vietnam War. My acquaintances received an invitation from the Chinese government to visit China, where Zhou Enlai received them. They were among the very first Americans allowed to go to China, and they considered themselves trailblazers. On their return to Hong Kong, they sang the praises of the new China and excitedly related what they had experienced. One fact that stuck in my mind was that the Chinese were so honest that they would chase after them to return small items left at hotels and money dropped on the ground. Since I knew so little about China, I had no idea what to think, except that this was a very different China from my imagination.

My boyfriend at the time, Jonathan Unger (to whom I am now married), was a stringer for the *Far Eastern Economic Review*. Shortly after our American acquaintances returned from their exciting trip, he managed to get himself invited to cover the Canton Trade Fair. He was the first American journalist ever to go. The day that he crossed the border into China, I thought: I don't want him to come out and tell me all that stuff about how good China is. I have to go to see it for myself. So I went to my Fourth Aunt, the one who was pro-China and had China contacts. She gave me the name and the address of a distant relative in Guangzhou, an old lady who was once the concubine of one of my great uncles. I did not tell my parents for fear they would object. I'd go for a couple of days.

I took the train to Lowu, the last station in Hong Kong before one enters China. I handed in my Hong Kong ID card at immigration on the Chinese side of the border. They would not let me pass. One officer after another came over to interrogate me: Why was I going to China? Why did you fill in "British subject," not "Chinese" in your ID card? I was dumbfounded, not knowing what I had filled in. Who are you going to see? They went through my address book and pointed to names and addresses, demanding to know who they were: Who is this person? Who is that person? The same questions were asked over and over again by different people. I was petrified. Never in my life had I encountered anything like this. In the end, they let me through. Even today, I do not know why I was singled out for questioning.

On the other side of the border, the panorama that greeted my eyes was the drab grayish hue of low-lying old houses interrupted by patches of red—flags and banners covered with slogans. The previous year, I had journeyed overland back to Hong Kong from Canada (I was an adventurous young woman), and I had seen very poor places in Turkey and Iran, but the scenery from the window of the Chinese train seemed oddly drab. It was a vast contrast from the colorful billboards and lights of Hong Kong.

I arrived at Guangzhou by nightfall and was able to find the old relative. She was a wizened old lady in a rundown shared house. She seemed alarmed to see me and nervous about our being seen together at the front door. She urged me inside and brought me to her tiny room, its walls blackened with age, with large water marks and a hole in the ceiling. She soon found an excuse to leave me there, and shortly afterward came back with someone in uniform. This person then took me somewhere in the neighborhood, sat me down, and began interrogating me. Much the same as at the border, several people fired the same questions at me again and again. I gradually realized I was at the *paichusuo*, the local police station.

The next scene I can recall was one of them bringing me to a dirty and unlit big room. I could make out there were beds with people sleeping in them. I was brought to a bed and was told this was where I had to spend the night.

The next morning it was decided that I was simply a young visitor from Hong Kong. I was escorted to a tricycle, and a man peddled me to a park, probably the Zhongshan (Sun Yatsen) Memorial Park. I walked around, not knowing much about Chinese history and not interested in being a "tourist" in this unwelcoming place nor in the prospect of spending another night in some grungy bed. I had seen enough. I headed back home.

My first trip to China lasted close to twenty-four hours. The China that I experienced was worse than what I had for years imagined. Now I could say to those American China experts and Jonathan Unger, the China I know is the real one.

An afterword: I happened to be in China at the height of the darkest days—the time of the One Hit and Three Antis Campaign. My distant relative, the old lady, must have been one of the five-bad-class-elements (*wuleifenzi*), and for the past two decades an easy and frequent target at class struggle sessions. My sudden appearance from nowhere could have brought calamity to her, for I was living evidence of her bourgeois "overseas" connections. My Fourth Aunt wore blinkers on her eyes, and my father, who knew so little about China, was after all right. Later, when I became a China specialist like my American acquaintances, the drab impoverished landscapes, the haranguing barrages of questions, the frightened look in the eyes of the old lady, and the awful tiny room she called home all contributed to my understanding of the underside of the Maoist period.

BROOM? SILK?

Perry Link

1973

My father was a history professor who became a devoted leftist during the Great Depression of the 1930s. My mother was the oldest daughter of German immigrants who ran a small family farm in Nebraska. I have met no one who fits the label "salt of the earth" better than my mother. Her name was Beulah, she ate wheat germ, and her favorite color was brown.

Without knowing it, she caused a problem in May 1973, during my first visit to China. I was on a one-month "thank-you" tour that China's government offered to me and eight others who had served, a year earlier, as interpreters for the Chinese Ping-Pong Delegation that had been an important harbinger of the diplomatic thaw between China and the United States. I set out for China full of excitement, goodwill, and a desire, born of my father's leftism as well as my own sharp criticisms of the U.S. war in Vietnam, to observe a socialist paradise in action.

One day, on a guided trip to a scenic spot near Hangzhou, I noticed a shop where small hand brooms were for sale. I thought of my mother. I had wanted to bring her a souvenir from China, and these brooms were perfect. They were crafted of sorghum stalks, light brown with dark flecks. Lovely. And symbols of the dignity of labor—which she and my father certainly would like. Imagining that she might hang it on a wall in their living room, I bought one.

As we boarded a minibus to return to our hotel, one of our guides made a point of sitting next to me. He appeared anxious—as if torn between handling an emergency and maintaining politeness.

"Why did you buy this?!" he asked.

I explained about my mother.

"Let me get you a better one!" He took the broom from my hand, went back to the shop, and soon returned with another—not much better or worse, to my eye, but in his view more nearly perfect. Then, during the ride back to the hotel, he began to interrogate me.

"Doesn't your mother like silk? . . . China has silk. China has jade carvings, China has cloisonné. Why do you buy a farmer's broom to represent China to your mother?" I began to realize that the guide saw what I had done as possibly "unfriendly." My mother and I were looking down on China.

For me, the misunderstanding raised a question that had not occurred to me before: Did this guide, deep inside, respect China's working people, the wielders of brooms—and want my mother to have the impression that "China is silk" only because he guessed that she, from a bourgeois society, would respect silk but not brooms? Or could the problem be deeper? Could it be that the ideal socialist society of my mind was more theory than reality? Could it be that Chinese people, including this guide, only pretended to value brooms over silk? The answer wasn't clear to me, but the question opened a window.

Two weeks later, our group was in Tangshan, in northeastern Hebei province, where we descended into the famous nearby coal mines. I noticed that, deep in the mines, there were signs for directions and safety, but no revolutionary slogans. In sharp contrast, on the earth's surface, quotations from Chairman Mao on bold red signs with white or gold letters were almost everywhere. I asked our guide why there were no Mao quotations down in the mines.

The suggestion caused her to scowl. "Too dirty!" she blurted.

Wheels began turning inside my slow mind. So: the dirt of the mines is all right for the working class, but not for the thoughts of its leader?

悟

WHERE ARE THE CHILD PSYCHOLOGISTS?

Martin King Whyte

1973

I was invited to be the "China expert" accompanying a delegation of American child psychologists that the Committee on Scholarly Communication with the People's Republic of China (CSCPRC) sent to China in November 1973. The trip allowed me to visit for the first time the country I had been studying from a distance for close to a decade. Although my discipline, sociology, had been abolished in China in 1952, psychology had survived within the Chinese Academy of Sciences on the grounds that it is partially a physical science. Chinese child psychologists had published some research articles in the 1950s, so it made sense that child psychology would be the field of the first CSCPRC social science delegation to China. I was not a child psychologist, but as a family sociologist, the CSCPRC apparently decided I was close enough. There were a dozen other members of the delegation, which was headed by William Kessen, a distinguished child psychologist at Yale. We entered China in the old-fashioned way, crossing the Lowu bridge on foot from Hong Kong and walking toward Shenzhen, then a sleepy train depot surrounded by farm fields, where we boarded a train for Guangzhou.

Early in our tour of five cities over three weeks, it became apparent that we and our Chinese hosts had some differing assumptions that were causing misunderstandings. We were immediately puzzled, for example, by the transportation protocol. Each morning as we set out, Bettye Caldwell, an accomplished but somewhat junior member of our delegation, rode in a sedan up front with local education officials, while the rest of us, including Bill Kessen, rode behind in a van. This happened, it turned out, because the CSCPRC had sent our hosts the names of our delegation in alphabetical order. The hosts assumed that Bettye, listed first, was our leader. When we explained that this was not the case (and expressed surprise that Maoist China was concerned with status rankings), Bettye was demoted to the van, and Bill Kessen took his rightful place in the lead sedan.

As we visited nursery schools and kindergartens in Guangzhou, my colleagues began to express frustration that we weren't seeing any primary or middle schools. This problem, it turned out, arose because the title of our group, "Childhood Education Delegation," had been translated as *youer jiaoyu daibiao tuan*—"Preschool Education Delegation." When we indicated that we wanted to see schools above the toddler level, our hosts rearranged our schedule for us.

Our hosts also adjusted our itinerary after we complained that we were going to visit coastal cities only. In response, they gave us Xi'an instead of Tianjin. The buried terra-cotta warriors at Xi'an had not yet been discovered, so for sightseeing we had to make do with a visit to the hot springs where Chiang Kai-shek had been kidnapped by Zhang Xueliang's troops in 1936. My enduring memory of Xi'an in 1973 is how people there were even less accustomed to seeing foreigners than were the people of Guangzhou and Beijing. At the Bell Tower in the center of the city, a few dozen people stopped to watch us as we began climbing up the stairs. By the time we reached the top and had begun to descend, more than a thousand people surrounded the Bell Tower, gawking up at us as if we were descending from Mars.

Another of my vivid impressions was the palpable anxiety and fear that lay just under the surface. This was understandable in view of the chaotic political campaigns in Mao's final years. On one occasion, for example, I was walking across the lobby of the old Beijing Hotel and noticed that on the crimson velvet draperies that lined the lobby walls, where Mao quotations in large white characters had once been displayed, the characters had been removed, but their indentations were still visible. I turned to our young guide and asked him what this removal meant. He replied, in a quavering voice, "I have no idea."

Another memory from that same lobby illustrates my great potential as a predictor of Chinese political trends. I had descended from my room one evening to buy some postcards. Wandering across the dimly lit lobby, I heard a noise off to my left and looked up at the large doors of a banquet hall atop a short flight of stairs. The doors swung open, and who should come walking out but the only-recently-rehabilitated Deng Xiaoping. He was followed some paces behind by Foreign Minister Qiao Guanhua, who was walking arm in arm with a visiting African head of state. Deng descended a few steps and then stopped and looked back over his shoulder at the other guests, who, ignoring him, were still in animated conversation. Deng looked forward again and continued down the steps, his white socks flopping down around his ankles. He proceeded out the front door and off into the night. I was too intimidated to say anything to him, but recall thinking to myself, "Well, Deng may have been officially rehabilitated after the Cultural Revolution, but clearly he is not going to have much influence."

A particularly dramatic demonstration of political fear came toward the end of our trip, in a meeting in our Shanghai hotel with leading education officials of that city. We had brought to China a four-volume set of the *Handbook of Child Psychology*, intending to present it as a gift to child psychologists we met. Bill Kessen had lugged the heavy tomes with us from city to city. In each we asked to meet with child psychologists but were always told that none were available. (Visitors to China in those years became familiar with the *meiyou*, "there aren't any," syndrome.) Finally, in Shanghai, Kessen demanded that child psychologists be produced because he was not going to carry the volumes back to the United States. Midway through the meeting, we were informed that two child psychologists, a man and a woman, had been found. They entered the room. Both were visibly quivering and, despite the mild temperature, sweating. From their appearance, we supposed that they might have been plucked out of a labor reform camp to come meet us. When we asked them what psychology theories they used, the man nervously responded that Marxism and class analysis were all they needed. Freud, Jung, and Piaget were irrelevant. They did take the four volumes off our hands, though, expressed thanks while looking down at the floor, and scurried out of the room. Ever since, I have puzzled over a simple question: What progress in Sino-American scholarly communication resulted from having two lonely child psychologists leafing through the *Handbook of Child Psychology* at night, after (as we imagined it) hard days of forced labor and mandatory thought reform?

THIRD-WORLD STUDENTS IN CHINA

Donald Clarke

1977

In the fall of 1977, I got to know a number of African students at the Beijing Languages Institute (BLI). They were a very friendly group, but on the whole seemed not terribly happy to be in China. The Ugandan students were particularly concerned because they had signed up for a degree program and had been told by the Ugandan Ministry of Education that that was what they were going to get, but on arriving in China discovered they would get only a diploma—not enough to qualify them for postgraduate studies anywhere. My diary entry from September 5, 1977, records the following:

> African students have a completely different worldview from second-worlders. We would give our eye-teeth to be here; most of them wanted to go to Europe to study. They applied for foreign study and got sent to China. They study technical subjects for 4 or 5 years after 1 or 2 years at the Beijing Languages Institute. We are willing to put up with Chinese

restrictions because we are so glad to be here. They see nothing special about going to China, hence chafe at bureaucratism. "Il n'y a pas de plaisir ici."

One day I went to visit a friend in the women's dormitory at BLI. While a few of us were in her room chatting with the door open, a young North Korean woman who lived on the same floor came by. It turned out she played the accordion, which was accordingly produced. Great—how about playing us a song? But please, we asked, make sure it's a song we all know. (I suppose we were thinking of something like "Red River Valley," which seems to be as ubiquitous in Asia as those red, white, and blue striped plastic carry bags, or young women making the V sign with both hands when being photographed.) No problem, she answered. She would play "The Song of General Kim Il-Sung." Hmm—awkward. "But we don't know that," we said. Her jaw dropped. "You don't?" She was genuinely shocked. Presumably she had grown up hearing that people around the world constantly had that song on their lips.

Part II

悟

Openings

The death of Mao Zedong on September 9, 1976, led to large changes in China. Within a month, four of Mao's closest associates—Zhang Chunqiao, Yao Wenyuan, Wang Hongwen, and Mao's wife Jiang Qing, known as the "Gang of Four"—were arrested, imprisoned, and scapegoated for many of the extremist policies that originally had been Mao's own. Mao's chosen successor, Hua Guofeng, was a weak leader who within months was maneuvered out of the top spot in China's ruling circles by Deng Xiaoping, a leader much stronger than Hua and far more practical than Mao. Under Deng, all of Chinese society seemed to uncurl and revert to earlier, more normal, patterns. An unusual society-wide consensus emerged for a time. People everywhere—urban and rural, old and young, from all social stations, and both inside and outside the Party—agreed on pursuing an exciting, if only vaguely understood, goal they called "modernization."

With almost breathtaking speed, Deng announced a series of major changes in policies toward intellectuals and education. In fall 1977, it was suddenly announced that admission to universities would be done by entrance examinations that measured academic merit, not political connections; intellectuals were reclassified, along with workers, farmers, and soldiers, as respectable members of the "working class"; and people who had been given "hats" (political labels) during the 1957–1958 Anti-Rightist Campaign were "de-hatted" (exonerated). Deng then pushed the slogan "Practice is the sole criterion for testing truth," whose unspoken but clear subtext was that absolute authority by one person, such as Mao, will no longer be practiced. "Scar literature," *which allowed writers an unprecedented (if still limited) freedom to describe Mao-era problems of poverty, corruption, political bullying, and violence, became feverishly popular among Chinese readers.*

Deng called his overall policy "reform and opening." The word "opening" meant, among other things, that Western students, scientists, scholars, and eventually business people, tourists, and others, would be welcome to come to China. On January 1, 1979, the United States and China established formal diplomatic relations, and the first groups of American students and scholars on a semi-official U.S.-China exchange program run by the CSCPRC arrived in China later that year. Some of our essayists in part II were part of that program, and others came to China in different capacities, as detailed below, but all experienced the same exciting ferment that was in the air at the time, and give a sense for what it was like to be a foreigner in China when being one was still very rare.

YOUNG JOURNALISTS

Stephen R. MacKinnon

1978–1981

From 1978 to 1981 my wife Janice Rachie MacKinnon (1943–1999) and I worked as "foreign experts" in China with our two children. My appointment was in the Journalism Institute at the newly created Chinese Academy of Social Sciences. But my real *danwei* (work unit) was the international department of the *People's Daily*. My job was to teach English to a group of thirty well-connected young men who were to be the newspaper's first generation of foreign correspondents in twenty years to be sent to English-speaking countries. Janice's appointment was with the Xinhua News Agency, polishing English-language dispatches.

After a year of living in the Friendship Hotel, a large compound in the northwest of the city that had been built in the 1950s to house Soviet advisers, we moved across the town, closer to our children's school, to a compound that was being rebuilt to be the new home of the *People's Daily*. The site had once been a university campus, but the school had been ravaged during the Cultural Revolution and was now abandoned. The buildings were in bad shape, used mostly for storage by the neighboring factory. Horses lived on the first floor of an old building in which my students lived, dormitory-style, on the second floor. We ate in a makeshift canteen in another dilapidated building. China's poverty was still apparent. There was a shortage of dairy products and, in winter, of vegetables. Basic commodities like rice were rationed. Hot running water in our flat was a luxury that was permitted only to us foreigners. (One result: we got visits from colleagues who drank tea and took a hot bath.) Ownership of bicycles, the only means of private transport, was rationed as well, and so on a number of occasions, given our privileged access, we bought bicycles for colleagues (with their money).

I met with my students almost daily for two years. They were a handpicked group of males in their late twenties who were from the families of high officials. I was told that they were chosen for their writing skills in Chinese and their rudimentary knowledge of English. They dressed like workers in ordinary, baggy, beat-up clothes. They were earning master's degrees from the Chinese Academy of Social Sciences while training with me to be foreign correspondents. At the same time, on alternate days, they went out on writing assignments for the *People's Daily*. Each student was assigned a senior correspondent as a mentor—many of whom I met. They included the philosopher journalist Wang Ruoshui and the investigative reporter Liu Binyan (both of whom were forced into exile by the events of June 4, 1989, and died in the United States). In later years, I was told that the 1979–1982 period was a "golden age" of reform and experimentation in Chinese journalism. A sad commentary, if true, on what came later.

In retrospect, considering the later trajectory of their careers, the most important member of the class was Bo Xilai, who is now languishing with a lifetime prison sentence after losing a power struggle for the top job to fellow princeling Xi Jinping, who is now chairman of the Party and president of the country. Bo Xilai's father was Bo Yibo, a legendary revolutionary general who had fought alongside Mao Zedong and Deng Xiaoping and who was still active in the late 1970s. At the time I taught Bo Xilai, he was the most prominent of the princelings in the class. He had just emerged from a factory where he had been shoveling coal after a stint in the countryside during the Cultural Revolution—a time when his mother had committed suicide and his father had been thrown into prison. He was tall and gawky—rather bony in appearance—with an oversize head. He had an engaging way of wagging his head with a smile. Socially, he fit in well with the others, careful to act like an ordinary member of the class. Although married with a son, he lived in the dorm during the week. Come the weekend, he returned to the high-walled, secretive compound for the elite of Beijing, known as Zhongnanhai, off Tiananmen Square. On one occasion, his connection to Zhongnanhai was useful to all of us. He turned up one hot summer weekend at a class picnic in the countryside with two cases of beer—which then was in very short supply and available in such quantity only from Zhongnanhai.

I met Bo every two or three years after we parted in 1982. He would always remind me of my opening lecture in 1979 on why and how "individualism" was a positive philosophical principle that underlay much of Western civilization. I remain amazed that my diatribe on individualism had made such a big impression. And I wonder, in retrospect, given the sad outcome of Bo's career, if it was individualism that landed him in prison for life.

Very few "foreign experts" were attached to the Chinese Academy of Social Sciences in those days, and this meant that people like me got invited to some extraordinary teas for newly recruited personnel. Many if not most of the scholars joining the academy were "rightists" who had been purged in the late 1950s and now had been exonerated and were returning from the provinces. Zhou Yang, who had been close to Mao and the Party's cultural czar since the 1930s, was now presiding over the academy, and Wang Guangmei, the wife of the former president Liu Shaoqi, was head of its Foreign Affairs Office. Mei Yi, head of Beijing radio before the Cultural Revolution, was Party secretary. It was a star-studded leadership cast.

I have a vivid memory of one of those teas. There were many tables and hundreds of senior scholars in attendance. I was seated next to Zhou Yang. Midway through the meeting, after several speeches, including a fiery one by eighty-five-year-old Chen Hansheng on what real social science is, Zhou went to the podium and began a long speech. He looked up occasionally at the assemblage before him. He knew many in the audience personally because earlier he had destroyed their lives. Over half of the group had been condemned by him as rightists in 1957. Later everybody, including Zhou Yang himself, had suffered terribly during the Cultural Revolution. His speech became more emotional as he continued, and his tone became more apologetic. Then suddenly he stopped, almost in midsentence.

He was in tears. He returned to his seat and grabbed my hand. He said nothing and held on to me for a long time. The audience was left hanging—silent and stunned, it seemed to me, that finally the great man had shown remorse in public.

悟

THE OPERATION OF POWER

Donald Clarke

1978

Two anecdotes can illustrate things I learned about the operation of power in China.

The first can be summed up as, "Ask forgiveness, not permission." I noticed it in 1977–1978 in the experience of a fellow Canadian student who was very interested in visiting old temple sites and other places of archaeological or artistic interest. At the time, Beijing and other Chinese cities had perimeters marked by signs that read *waiguoren zhibu*: "No foreigners beyond this point." The sites this student wanted to see were usually beyond the perimeters. He may have intuited that any request for permission to visit would be turned down; a "yes" answer would have entailed the assignment of someone to accompany him and to take the heat if anything ever went wrong—and no one would want that assignment. He may actually have tried asking permission and found it hard to get. In any case, he adopted the solution of simply ignoring the signs. When caught, he humbly admitted his error, promised not to do it again, and then did it again a while later, each time humbly apologizing once more. The school authorities tolerated, and perhaps even admired, this technique. At year's end, he was cited as a model "Three Good" student (good in virtue, knowledge, and physique).

The second anecdote is about the important distinction between form and substance. On May 4, 1978, the whole of Peking University turned out for a ceremony marking the eightieth anniversary of the university's founding. Zhou Peiyuan, a distinguished seventy-six-year-old physicist, was about to be formally installed as president of

Peking University. Zhou delivered remarks that we foreign students had been admonished to listen to carefully and in silence. Right up there with him on the rostrum was the Party secretary, Zhou Lin, who was a tough old bird, aged sixty-six at the time, who had been involved in political and security work for the Party before 1949 and had been through various political ups and downs (who hadn't?) in the years after. Throughout Zhou Peiyuan's speech, Zhou Lin was chatting away with the person beside him. Not only was the chatting visible to everyone, but as the microphone in front of him was still on, it was also audible to everyone—not comprehensibly, but rather as a kind of drone accompanying the melody. I vaguely sensed what was going on at the time—in any case, I found it worth writing about in my diary—but by now I have read enough anthropology to see more clearly what it was all about: Zhou Lin was signaling, not just to Zhou Peiyuan but to everyone, who was really the boss even before the new university president was formally in place.

THE REHABILITATION OF SOCIOLOGY

Martin King Whyte

1979

After the post-Mao reforms were launched, the American Council of Learned Societies and Social Science Research Council decided to send a delegation to China to gather information about plans for reviving social science and humanities disciplines, which had been decimated under Mao. I was asked to join the delegation, and Burt Pasternak (anthropology, Hunter College) and I were assigned to investigate plans for the revival of sociology and anthropology, which in China are lumped together as *sociology*.

Soon after our delegation arrived in Beijing in December 1979, Burt and I were driven to a large meeting hall where we were to spend an entire day hearing reports about plans to "rehabilitate" sociology. When we entered the hall, we were warmly greeted by several dozen surviving sociologists and anthropologists, all in their sixties, seventies, and eighties. In the morning session, Fei Xiaotong, who had received a British anthropology PhD in the 1930s and was now president of the newly established Chinese Sociological Research Association, presided over a wide-ranging review of the plans for sociology. We knew that during the 1956 Hundred Flowers Campaign, Fei had led a failed effort to have the ban on sociology, imposed in 1952, lifted. Now he was getting another chance.

In the afternoon, the floor was turned over to Lin Yaohua, holder of a 1940 Harvard anthropology PhD and a leading professor in the Central Nationalities Academy. Lin launched into a parallel discussion of plans for the future of ethnology (*minzuxue*, research on China's national minorities). As Lin started speaking, the atmosphere in the hall became noticeably tense. Everyone in the hall knew, as did Burt and I, that Fei and Lin hated each other, and with good reason. In 1957, Lin Yaohua was the leading critic of Fei Xiaotong during the Anti-Rightist Campaign when Fei was labeled a rightist and condemned to political and professional purgatory for twenty years. We also all knew that in the early 1970s, after Fei was partially rehabilitated, he had to work in ethnology under the control of his denouncer. When Fei was allowed to meet with a visiting American anthropologist in 1972 (with Lin in attendance), he was obliged to renounce all of his earlier work and to declare that sociology and anthropology were not needed because they were "disciplines under the control of bourgeois ideology." Now, seven years later, Fei was exulting in his opportunity to escape from the confines of ethnology and the clutches of Lin Yaohua and spearhead the revival of sociology. It was equally clear that Lin was very resentful at being left behind in the sterile backwater of ethnology. Burt and I concluded that if the political wheel turned again, Lin would be only too eager to lead another attack on Fei.

As if this were not enough drama for one day, more was to come. As the meeting was concluding, I was approached by Lei Jieqiong, who had received an American sociology MA in the 1930s and was now slated for a leading role in the yet-to-be-established Department of Sociology at Peking University. She asked to meet with me privately in my room in the Beijing Hotel at 7:00 p.m. to provide more details on the plans for sociology. I readily agreed, but that evening, 7:00 p.m. passed and no Professor Lei appeared. Finally, after 7:30, she knocked loudly on my door. When she came in, she was furious and almost in tears. She told me that when she arrived at the hotel, security guards would not let her enter. She protested angrily that, among her other titles, she was currently a vice mayor of Beijing, and since the Beijing Hotel fell under city administration, she had every right to enter. But the guards stood their ground, and it took further extended arguments and appeals to higher authorities before they finally relented and allowed her in. Our conversation during the remainder of her visit was as much about the idiocy of Chinese bureaucracy as about the prospects for sociology. (Fortunately, Chinese sociology revived and has flourished since, despite its rocky relaunch.)

Later in that trip, I had another illuminating experience that had nothing to do with sociology. After a dinner banquet in Shanghai, some of our group decided to walk back to our hotel. As we set off after 9:30, the streets were very dimly lit. We saw only an occasional lonely bicyclist or late-night bus. It seemed that the entire population of Shanghai was already home for the night, if not asleep. As we approached a major intersection we saw something peculiar. Several dozen middle-aged and older women were lined up on both sides of the cross street and across the intersection, spaced about ten feet apart. A policeman was out in the street, directing the women where to stand. Ever the nosy American, I went up to the policeman and asked, "What are these women doing?" Unhappy seeing foreigners, he responded brusquely, "They are not doing anything!" Stymied by his angry but technically accurate answer, we turned left and continued on down the same street.

Perhaps ten minutes later, we heard a sound and turned to see a cortege of black limousines speeding past us. It was not until the next morning that we understood what we had viewed. An important Japanese trade delegation had arrived on a late flight at the old Hongqiao airport, and the limousines were whisking them to their hotel. Apparently, the Shanghai authorities were worried that some residents might remember Japanese war atrocities in 1937 and come out to throw rocks at the cars of the visiting Japanese, thus disrupting current Sino-Japanese relations. So they had the police notify residents' committees along the route that the Japanese would be traveling by, telling them to mobilize the nighttime sentries we had observed, just to be on the safe side. We joked among ourselves that, even if Jesus Christ were to make his second coming in Boston or New York, it was hard to imagine that local residents could be rousted from their beds at night in this fashion in order to guarantee his safe arrival.

悟

A NIGHT WITH THE POST OFFICE GUYS

James M. Hargett

1979

In June 1979, I had just completed a Fulbright year in Taiwan and was getting ready to head back to the United States to complete my PhD dissertation when an unexpected letter from the U.S. State Department arrived in my Taibei mailbox. I had taken the Foreign Service Examination the year before so guessed the letter might be asking me to travel to Washington, D.C., for further testing or something like that. I was wrong. The letter was a handwritten note from Steve Holder, a former classmate at Indiana University:

> Hargett—I am now working at the U.S. Embassy in Beijing. If you want to come for a visit, I can make the necessary arrangements. Send me a telegram from Hong Kong if you are interested.

To this day, I do not know how Holder found my apartment address on Linyi Street in Taibei. In any case, it was not long before I was on a plane to Hong Kong. The official invitation—printed on U.S. Embassy stationery—arrived a day or two later. After getting a visa through a local travel service, I was on an evening flight from Guangzhou to Beijing. What happened next changed my life forever.

Before the United States and China established formal diplomatic relations on January 1, 1979, China was essentially "off limits" to my generation of China scholars. Some of my classmates at Indiana University did their dissertation research in Taiwan or Japan, and some never left the United States. As a result, many of my classmates, without meaning any disrespect, developed only limited speaking skills in modern Chinese. I was different because of my family background in Taiwan and my intensive study of Chinese for two consecutive summers at Middlebury College. Yet in 1979, I still felt, in a sense, that my language skills were "untested" because I had never set foot in Mainland China. I had communicated well with friends and teachers in Taiwan but now would face new language challenges such as heavy regional accents, local and colloquial expressions (*tuhua*), and unfamiliar dialects.

It was around midnight when Holder picked me up at the Beijing airport, and we both were hungry.

"How about some beer and dumplings?" he asked.

"Sounds good to me!" I replied.

After a short drive, we arrived at a non-elite dumpling house. It was packed with workers from the local post office, who had just gotten off their shift. Holder was one of the most gregarious people I have ever known, and he immediately engaged several of the workers in conversation. One of his favorite pastimes was memorizing lengthy passages from Sunzi's *The Art of War*. His performance that night had soon mesmerized an audience of at least one hundred workers who had crowded around us. I suspect that most of them had no idea what he was saying. It didn't matter. The only thing that mattered was that he was a foreigner reciting something that was Chinese. Afterward, one of the workers asked if I, too, could recite something. I rattled off Su Shi's (1037–1101) "First Prose-Poem on the Red Cliff," which I had once memorized for a speech contest at Middlebury.

It would be an understatement to say that Holder and Hargett were big "entertainment hits" that night. We talked with the workers until dawn. Many of them told us they had never met a foreigner before. Holder and I replied that we had never drunk beer out of soup bowls before. Everyone laughed as we ended and went our separate ways.

When I recall that night when Holder and I drank beer out of soup bowls and ate plate after plate of dumplings, I am astonished at how well our teachers had prepared us for that "night with the post office guys" in Beijing. There was no language barrier; there was no reluctance to ask or answer almost any question (several of the workers wanted to know why Richard Nixon was forced to resign; one guy even asked, "Isn't it normal for political leaders to spy on their enemies"?). Holder and I were different from the workers in almost every respect, and yet everyone communicated without hesitation or difficulty. I am still amazed at how differences in cultures, lifestyles, and experiences can be bridged by a common spoken language. If only the politicians of the world would spend more time learning foreign languages.

I dedicate this happy reminiscence to my classmate and friend Stephen Galbraith Holder (1947–2016).

悟

STAMP CONNECTIONS

Wendy Larson

1979

I started collecting stamps in Walla Walla, Washington, when I was eleven years old. My dad had given me his album, which he assembled as a youngster in Portland, Oregon, and told me how he would scrimp to buy stamps by walking miles to the stamp shop. My only stamp-collecting friend lived in the tiny town of Milton-Freewater, just across the border in Oregon. The primitive pre-Internet environment did not prevent us from pursuing our hobby avidly. Checking ads in comic books and magazines, we would send away for bundles of used stamps, numbering in the thousands but costing under a dollar per packet, and happily organize them in our albums. We used the now-defunct method of small paper hinges with glue on them, which was an improvement over earlier practices of simply pasting the stamps into books. We didn't pay much attention to history. Some of it sank in nonetheless, and I learned that China was Taiwan, and the PRC was "red" China.

In Europe and the United States, stamp collecting was popular among men, women, and children in the 1800s. In the twentieth century, as the focus moved toward interest in printing, perforations, and watermarks, the hobby became dominated by men, who approached it from a technical perspective. I had been a sporadic collector before I arrived in China in 1979 when, for some reason, I picked it up again, probably because collecting stamps was still widely popular in China. Today, Chinese collecting has driven an impressive increase in the value of Chinese stamps, with Qing Dynasty stamps and revolutionary themes being very much in demand.

In the fall of 1979, an exhibition of all Chinese stamps produced since 1949 was traveling around China. The organizers encouraged viewers to submit ballots on what they regarded as the best stamp sets, with no criteria to define quality. I biked to the exhibition hall and, after viewing and reading about the stamps and their histories, submitted five ballots. I made my choices on principles I no longer thoroughly recall, but they included a set of politically important stamps as well as one based on the stamps I liked best, which usually were single-color engraved pieces.

I often went to the "stamp corner" in Beijing to trade with local collectors, but found myself in over my head with traders who knew a lot more than I did. Most of my Chinese stamps came from fellow students at Peking University. Several gave me small collections that included stamps from the Cultural Revolution. As one friend explained, the political winds could shift rapidly, and no one knew if the Cultural Revolution might once again get wings, or if a radical anti-revolutionary movement would develop. If someone was caught with a questionable collection, the consequences would be unpredictable. But throwing the stamps away was also dangerous, especially if they bore pictures of Mao Zedong or other revolutionary leaders. Therefore, giving stamps to a foreign collector who studied China seemed like a good solution. I also collected Mao badges—which were gratefully handed over for similar reasons—and was touched when I was given collections organized not historically, technically, or with an eye to preserving value, but based on nothing more than youthful passion.

One day I was surprised when the woman who managed our dorm entry and telephone access rushed up to tell me that I was one of about fifteen national winners. Although there had been no objective criteria on which to base one's vote, it turned out that "the people" chose which stamps were best, and only a small number of participants managed to select all of those favored stamps. It was something like a lottery. According to notes I took at the time, the winner was the set I had chosen just because I liked them. Winning based on my personal taste suggested to me that I was in sync with the People. That vindicated me, especially in light of what some other foreign students at the university had told me: that my collecting was antithetical to socialism and showed a bourgeois disrespect for the spiritual values of Maoism.

I later learned that in the 1950s and early 1960s, the national stamp-collecting journal *China Philately* (*Zhongguo jiyou*) had published many articles debating the relationship between socialism and collecting. Collecting anything—art, stamps, Mao badges, artifacts—for the wrong reasons was thoroughly discouraged. These reasons included ideological aspects such as trying to collect stamps from capitalist countries for their relative rarity and unusual value. Another unrevolutionary aspect of collecting was competitiveness and lack of cooperation among collectors, which apparently was a problem as early as the 1950s.

I was invited to contribute an article to *China Philately*. After it was published, I received hundreds of letters and stamps from all over China. I tried to respond to the letters but was quickly overwhelmed. Often many pages long, the letters detailed more than just collecting. They told how people had lived their lives and what kinds of problems they had encountered. They expressed a desire to connect with people outside China through stamp collecting, which to many seemed a way to transcend political differences. As someone named Ren from Hunan wrote,

> I was a passionate Chinese youth, but my young intellectual life was destroyed. History will be my judge. I wanted to go to university and be a scientist, but a different route unfolded. In 1965 when I graduated from middle school, the trouble had just begun. I had no choice but to give up my hopes of going to high school, instead going to the countryside to work. Then there were ten years of revolution and my ideals were destroyed.

Severely nearsighted, Ren struggled to find work after the Cultural Revolution was over. His girlfriend abandoned him, the factory where he finally got a job would not treat his illnesses, and he ended up living on his parents' retirement income. He hoped to learn English by becoming my pen pal.

Collectors all over China regarded my short article in *Jiyou* as a door cracked open. Apologizing for their brashness in writing as a stranger, they hoped to exchange stamps and have an American friend. When I was ready to go back to school in the United States, I bundled up the letters and took them to the Friendship Store, which was the only place where foreigners could arrange for shipping their belongings home. Usually, everything was checked carefully. I was worried that my stamps would be confiscated, so I hid them among other papers and journals. They arrived intact. I always imagine that the day will come when I will have time to write back to each person who took the risk of writing to me, a foreigner, and send them some stamps from the United States in appreciation of their generosity and bravery.

BUYING SOCKS

Perry Link

1979

During 1979–1980, my wife and I lived on the campus of Zhongshan University on the outskirts of Guangzhou. Comrades from the Foreign Affairs Office were assigned to help us do whatever it was we needed to do, but the tedium of requesting the help—and then waiting for it—sometimes grew burdensome. The application for help in doing X was taking more work than doing X would.

One day I wanted to buy socks and made the appropriate application for assistance.

"We'll study it," came the reply.

After a few days I followed up.

"Well?"

"We're studying it. We're trying to arrange a car for you."

"I don't need a car. I can go myself, by bus or bike."

I owned a Flying Pigeon bicycle, because the comrades in the Foreign Affairs Office had applied for and received the authority to allow me to buy one outside the rationing system. Anybody else who wanted a bicycle needed a ration coupon. I looked at my bike and thought: Hey, why not just hop on and go buy the socks myself? I know where the department store is, and I know the roads.

So I did that. Later I confided in a friend, a young professor in the Chinese Department.

"I hope I didn't upset the Foreign Affairs people."

"You did the opposite," he said. "You let them relax."

"Hunh?" I didn't get it.

He explained: "When you make an official request, they have to make an official decision on it. If they officially say 'yes' and then something goes wrong, they will be officially responsible. That's a bit frightening to them, so they ask instruction from the next highest level. Then if something goes wrong, the blame goes to that level, not to them. Your request for permission to buy socks may have gone up pretty far—and that's why it took time."

"Wow."

"But if you just go do it, without their permission, they don't have to take responsibility. So they relax."

悟

A SINGLE ROOM

Vera Schwarcz

1979

I don't know what possessed me to break the rules in early March 1979, when I was getting ready to move into the dorms at Peking University. Some of these rules were unwritten, yet I felt compelled to articulate them to myself, and then to defy them, if possible. The written ones, like the signs that warned "Out of Bounds for Foreigners Without Special Permits" (in English, Chinese, and Russian), I had already challenged by wandering by myself into the mountains behind Yiheyuan, the Summer Palace. What I was about to defy was not so much a Chinese regulation as a Western assumption about how to get to know China in those early days of scholarly exchanges.

The axiom among my fellow American students (sent in the first small group of exchange scholars in February 1979) was that we would fight to have Chinese roommates. That was assumed to be the key to getting "inside"—to knowing the underside of Chinese social life, which was still hard to glimpse in an era of shaky recovery from the Cultural Revolution. For some reason, I asked for a single room. In the days before I was approved to enter Peking University (while other American students stayed sequestered at the Foreign Languages Institute), I decided I would *not* ask for a Chinese roommate.

Maybe because I grew up in communist Romania in shared housing, I had a stronger thirst for solitude than the other Americans. My fellow exchange students all wanted "in" and here I was betraying the cause by wanting "out." This was a traitorous path when the entire goal of our mission as pioneers in the exchange process was to push for every avenue of access into Chinese life and scholarly community.

Yet I sensed that it was more than a craving for privacy that made me put forth the audacious request for a single room. I had a wordless intuition that *dandu*, "single," would pay off in ways that I could not fathom in the blustery and dust-filled air of Beijing in March 1979. A compound concept suggesting dogs, vermin, and unsociability, *dandu* was going to be my goal, come hell or high water.

"Singleness" was not a useful idea in Beijing at that time. The Foreign Office at the university agreed very reluctantly to grant me a single room because I was the most "senior" of the exchange group—I had a PhD already in hand. Fellow Americans were convinced I had blown the best opportunity in this new era of "friendship" with China. I persisted on this crazy course of action.

After I moved in on March 12, 1979, I decorated my small room in Dormitory 25 (the women's one, with squat toilets, hot water for showers once a week and about a hundred Chinese undergraduates sharing rooms in groups of six and eight) with conscious effort: First I bought three plants in coarse clay pots, at a time when such "luxuries" were not common. I needed *qi* (air) in claustrophobic times. On one wall, I hung a Romanian folk cloth (what made me bring it from the United States, this tiny remnant of my old home?) to alert my guests that although I was here as an official "American" exchange scholar, my own roots were elsewhere, closer to China's communist culture.

On the other wall, I put a small, cheap scroll of Lu Xun's famous saying that I bought at the local bookshop: "Head-bowed, like a willing ox I serve the children." This washed well with school authorities who came to visit me weekly. I can't remember if I did not find or did not choose to put up the first part of Lu Xun's sentence: "Fierce-browed, I coolly defy a thousand pointing fingers." But that's what I was doing—defying accusatory fingers.

My rebellion paid off handsomely. Without a roommate and with two single iron beds framing a small desk, I was able to host Chinese teachers and friends every day, every hour. We were "alone," *dandu*—even as we knew that we were watched, heard, commented upon. But behind closed doors, a breath of intimate sharing developed over time. As my spoken language skills improved, I managed to listen more and more to silences, to what lay between words.

When I moved into the dormitory, I had no idea that I would be doing oral history for the next two decades. I could not have imagined all the doors for interviews that would open in the late 1980s. By that time, I had left behind my snug, single room in the dilapidated dormitory and was now hosted in the new guest center called Shao Yuan.

But looking back, I see that it all started with a risky choice: Not jumping into the "inside" of Chinese social life with a roommate, I ended up choosing otherness, outsiderness. This enabled me to listen in a different way to Chinese voices, and to my own as a writer in a language far from my native tongue. Only in China, only at Peking University did I finally understand the meaning of the overused poem by Robert Frost, "The Road Not Taken":

> Two roads diverged in a wood, and I—
> I took the one less traveled by,
> And that has made all the difference.

Sometimes you have to travel far to see your own world afresh. China gave me that blessing in 1979, and again and again for the next four decades, until today.

悟

DEATH OF A TOURIST

Morris Rossabi

1979

In February of 1979, a travel agency recruited me to lead a trip to China, one of the first such tours for Americans. The tour group, which included the distinguished sinologist Chauncey Goodrich of the University of California, Santa Barbara, was convivial and sophisticated and responded to my lectures with fine questions and comments. The trip was expensive and required medical certification that the traveler could undertake what was labeled an "arduous journey." It turned out to be less physically demanding than advertised, and the two Chinese guides were solicitous and ensured that the tour did not pose insuperable physical obstacles.

The trip went smoothly until we reached Shanghai. We saw all the sites we requested in Beijing, Xi'an, and Luoyang and were permitted to spend as much time as we wanted at especially intriguing locations. At this point, I noticed that a member of the group had a bad cough that appeared to be worsening. In Xi'an, I had asked him if he wanted me to arrange a visit to a clinic or a hospital. He responded that he was grateful for my concern, but that he had the proper medicines to control his illness. When we reached Shanghai, however, he appeared to be even more distressed. After our first supper in Shanghai, he knocked on my door and said that he had to return to the United States. I pointed out that we could set up an appointment at a clinic, but he was adamant about his desire to go home.

Fulfilling his wish was no easy task. We were traveling on a group visa, which entailed entering and exiting China as a unit of twenty-six. The following day, while the rest of the group continued its tour of Shanghai, one of our guides and I devoted most of the day at public security offices to secure an individual visa for our ailing member. By late afternoon, we were successful, and the sick member departed for Guangzhou that evening and would fly home early the next morning. After a rather strenuous day, the guide and I had a wonderful banquet and complimented ourselves on the outcome.

The next morning, right after breakfast, I heard a knock on my door. The assistant director of Shanghai's China Travel Service requested that I get dressed and pack my belongings because I needed to fly to Guangzhou. Our tour member did not merely have a bad cough and cold. He had collapsed and died at the Guangzhou airport an hour or so before he was scheduled to depart for the United States. The assistant director drove me to the Shanghai airport where I boarded a plane on which I was one of only two passengers. From this point on, Chinese officials were extraordinarily efficient. There had been a few mistakes on the tour, but their performance from here on was flawless.

On the verge of a boom for the tourist industry, Chinese officials were concerned about the death of a tourist and did not wish to be blamed for his demise. They feared that Chinese tourism would suffer considerable harm if doubts existed about safety in China. They immediately added several guides and other assistants to the group that remained in Shanghai and practically carried the members so that no one else would fall ill. At the same time, the authorities in Guangzhou, both from the Travel Service and the Communist Party, wanted me to approve an autopsy. I responded that I could not do so without approval from the family. They demanded that I call the family and specified clearly that I would remain in China until the issues relating to the death were resolved. Looking through the dead man's papers, I found a telephone number for his wife. At that time, international telephone services were still cumbersome and had to be booked in advance, but after some time, I was able to place a call to his wife. I gently described what had happened and was surprised by the response. His wife was afflicted by Alzheimer's and did not understand the sad news.

I needed a telephone number for another member of his family, but the travel agency, perhaps the principal source for such information, was closed because of Presidents' Day. The agency had not provided me with an emergency telephone number, and I, a novice at such activities, had not asked for one. The United States still did not have an embassy in China, which usually took charge if an American citizen died. I was on my own, and lacking an alternative, called my wife, hoping that she could obtain a telephone number for a family member. She called the Department of State and the Red Cross and, when I called again, had finally secured the number for the dead man's son. I reached the son, but he was reluctant to approve an autopsy. In despair, I mentioned that he would have to travel to China to deal with the authorities, and then he relented and sanctioned an autopsy. I transmitted the message to the Chinese authorities, who were delighted and treated me to another fabulous Chinese banquet.

About 2:00 a.m., I heard a knock on my door. It could not be a dream because I had resisted my Chinese hosts and had drunk only one and a half glasses of wine. I opened the door and faced an obviously angry official who asked why I had not told them about the radioactive pellets (a treatment for cancer) that were implanted in the dead man's body. He implied that the pathologists at the autopsy had been exposed to radiation, and he demanded that I find out how many such pellets had been implanted. Once again, I called the son and asked him why he had not told me about the pellets. He said that he had forgotten, but he provided me with the information that I needed. I now realized that the deceased had been so desperate to visit China that he risked his life to undertake the journey and did not reveal his illness in the medical forms.

The authorities now had additional requests. First, they asked me to check the dead man's belongings, including his cash and traveler's checks, to ensure that nothing was amiss. They did not wish to be accused of theft. Second, they insisted that I identify the body and drove me to what turned out to be a crematorium. I had never actually seen a dead body and though I did not faint, I was startled. Third, they sought approval for cremation, which again required a telephone call to the son. I faced difficulties at this point because the Chinese hotels demanded payment in cash for international telephone calls, and I was rapidly running out of money. Nonetheless, I called the son, who again hesitated but eventually relented and gave permission. I breathed a sigh of relief because I appeared to have completed all the arrangements.

To my surprise, however, the China Travel Service and the local Communist Party planned a memorial service as soon as the rest of the tour group joined us in Guangzhou. Even more surprising, they commissioned me to write a memorial speech in honor of the tourist whom I barely knew. I spent the rest of the day puzzling out a speech. The group arrived in Guangzhou that night, and the next morning we drove to the memorial hall, which had been festooned with flowers and plants. Each of us was given a black crepe armband to wear, and the authorities had taken the dead man's passport photo, which did not provide the optimal image, blown it up to a huge size, and placed it right in front of the memorial hall. After grand speeches by the secretary of the Communist Party in Guangzhou and the director of the local China Travel Service, I read my speech, part of which I copy here:

> Over the past few days, I have wondered why Mr. XX came to China. Knowing that he was gravely ill, what prompted him to go so far away from his home? We shall, of course, never know. . . . I suggest that, like Mr. XX, we wish to transcend our ordinary lives. . . . In our homes, the humdrum, the petty ensnare us. We worry about the grocery bills, our children's education, our possessions. Travel liberates us, detaches us from our possessions, . . . enables us to extend our vision. . . . I believe this is what Mr. XX must have cherished. He sought to expose himself to universal concerns and was not simply interested in his own small corner of the world. He was eager, on this trip, to find out about traditional China and the transformations that have been wrought over the past thirty years. Last Wednesday, he told me how much he had been impressed by the magnificent architectural monuments we had seen and, at the same time, by the concern and kindness we had been accorded by our Chinese hosts.

> We also travel in order to think of ourselves as part of a world community. We try to identify with other people and to know that we share characteristics with other members of the human race, be we Melanesians, Americans, Poles, Chinese, or Arabs. . . . The French poet Baudelaire has expressed this idea felicitously. Even while castigating his

critics and accusers, he writes, "Hypocrite lecteur, mon semblable, mon frère" (Hypocritical reader, my likeness, my brother). . . . We are, to use a trite but perhaps true expression, brothers under the skin. Here again, Mr. XX recognized this. He was aware of the many similarities between the Chinese people and the American people. Both of our peoples are hardworking, lively, and dedicated, but we also have marvelous senses of humor.

Mr. XX was happy throughout his stay in China because he had achieved his lifelong dream. Thus, though his death is a source of great sorrow for his family, for our group, and for our Chinese hosts, we should take heart that he himself was happy during his last days. . . . I think that Mr. XX would be pleased that he reached China on the verge of the initiation of diplomatic relations between our two countries. And I believe that he would join with us in hoping for peace and friendship between Americans and Chinese for ten thousand years and more.

My responsibilities did not end with this speech. At the Guangzhou railroad station on our way to Hong Kong, a China Travel Service representative handed me an urn with ashes from the cremation, which I delivered to the travel agency at the Los Angeles airport to be transmitted to the family.

The son never tried to reach me.

DONALD CLARKE

Bureaucracy and Nosiness

1977–1979

Five examples:

1. One of the British students at the Beijing Languages Institute (BLI) got transferred after a few months to Peking University. Whenever a Chinese friend of his from BLI tried to telephone him at his Peking University dorm, the *shifu* (the man who sits in a little booth guarding the entrance to buildings and answers the telephone) would insist on interrogating him with the standard set of questions everyone knew well: *Ni naer? Ni shenme danwei?* "Where are you calling from? What's

your work unit?" ("Where?" in questions like this meant much more than geographical location. It was more about social location: Who are you? What's your background? Why should I do anything for you?) As often as not, the *shifu* just hung up the telephone.

2. When two friends of mine—fellow students at Nanjing University in 1978–1979—applied to the school authorities in the early 1980s for permission to get married, the authorities were suspicious. "What's your *mudi* (object or goal)?" they asked. To realize how silly this is, you have to understand that in PRC Chinese, *mudi* can be—and in this case was—said with a certain inflection that makes it sound like a sinister plot.

3. The Foreign Affairs Office at Nanjing University came down hard on a Chinese student because her foreign roommate had thrown a birthday party for her. They called the Chinese student in and interrogated her: "Why did your roommate throw a birthday party for you?" Something highly irregular, perhaps sinister, had happened.

4. Whenever a foreign friend boarded a crowded bus in the late 1970s, the conductor would make someone yield his or her seat. This was of course completely unwanted and highly embarrassing to any of us young students, who—whether or not we were committed True Believers—all felt that this kind of special treatment was inappropriate. My own memory of the most ridiculous incident of this kind was when I boarded a bus in Beijing and witnessed the conductor require an old lady to give up her seat to me. There was absolutely no way I was going to take that seat, despite the urgings of the conductor and other passengers. And of course, the original occupant was not about to pull a Rosa Parks herself. So the seat stayed empty until the next stop, when a newly boarded passenger unfamiliar with the history spotted the empty seat, thanked his lucky stars, and sat down. On another occasion a man carrying a baby was ordered to get up and yield his seat to me. I got him to sit back down only by claiming that I was about to get off anyway.

5. Bureaucratic formulas sometimes allowed a bit of reprieve. My roommate in Nanjing told me that in April 1976, when Deng Xiaoping fell from grace by orders from the top and was dismissed from all his posts, he and his high school classmates were all required to write essays criticizing Deng. But nobody's heart was really in it. For those who didn't care to write such an essay, the school authorities permitted them to copy out an anti-Deng editorial from the *People's Daily* and to read it aloud.

Part III

悟

Stop Overexciting the Masses!

The effervescence in China's political mood during the late 1970s—and the happy consensus across state and society that "modernization" was the country's main goal—began to simmer down in 1980. Wei Jingsheng, the Beijing electrician who had called for democracy as a "fifth modernization" (the first four being Deng Xiaoping's modernization of agriculture, industry, national defense, and science and technology), was arrested and in October 1979 sentenced to fifteen years in prison. Beginning in 1980, writers of "scar literature" were counseled not to go so far as to challenge the current political system.

Deng Xiaoping did continue with "reform and opening" as his ruling mantra, however, and for most of the 1980s, a push and pull between "release" and "retrenchment" alternated in Chinese political and social life. This "reform" system was fairly stable, and still far more open than the Mao years, so young Western scholars, journalists, and business people continued to come into China.

悟

NO SIGNS, NO MAPS

Charlotte Furth

1981

In fall 1981, I began teaching at Peking University under the U.S. government's Fulbright program, which only recently had arrived in China after normalization of U.S.-China diplomatic relations in 1979. The offices and classrooms for our Fulbright group were housed in a grimly functional cement-block structure formerly dedicated to Russian-language studies and still known as the "R" building. The classrooms, with their high ceilings, unwashed casement windows, and cement walls and floors, made it feel a little bit like teaching at the bottom of a well. The few ancient steam radiators mounted around the walls suggested that the volume of enclosed air would never be warmed enough to allow us to shed our outer clothing in winter.

Except for this building and the library, where the officials in charge of our Fulbright group had their offices, the rest of the campus, and its faculty and students, were so many blank walls to me. There were no maps or guides to the grounds. Buildings were marked by numbers only, and office doors, which normally were shut, bore no names of their occupants. I never saw a class schedule, either for our group or for any other department at the university. If you belonged within this maze, you already knew what you needed to know. If you did not belong, you did not need to know.

Here is an example of what happened to me when, occasionally, I tried to explore beyond my assigned place. At a reception at the U.S. Embassy, I had been introduced to a Peking University history professor named Qi Wenying, who specialized in colonial America and could help me connect with the university's history program. The professor was visibly disappointed at my poor spoken Chinese but invited me to audit her class. It might be good language practice for me, I agreed. I went to the class at the appointed time. No one was there. A student saw me, told me that the class had been changed to Saturday afternoon, and then suggested that I try the History Department office. "It's in the second courtyard." I went. One unmarked door along the corridor was ajar, and an old man inside was busy writing. As I was hesitating about whether to disturb him, a woman came along the corridor. I told her I was looking for Professor Qi's office. "Can't you reach her at home?" she asked. I said I didn't have an address. The woman went into the open office and asked the old man my question. It turned out he was the staff assistant for the department and, after some suspicious looks, said he would take a note from me to Qi at her home in the faculty housing quarter. But it was now noon, he said, and time for lunch and a siesta. Would I come back with my note at two o'clock? Wandering around campus to kill time, I happened upon a student of mine who, learning of my predicament, said, "I will find Professor Qi and deliver your note." It would be easy, she said. "This afternoon is political study, and everyone will be on campus." I wrote my note and gave it to her. The next day she reported back that she had been unable to find Qi, so had taken the note to the History office, where she had also learned that the time change for Qi's class was for one week only. Eventually I gave up trying to audit Professor Qi's class. It was an activity outside my prescribed channel. Personally, Qi was nice to me; at Thanksgiving she invited me to her tiny apartment for a dumpling dinner.

悟

STOP OVEREXCITING THE MASSES!

Thomas D. Gorman

1980

One of the many fruits of the normalization of U.S.-China diplomatic relations in January 1979 was an agreement to exchange national trade and economic exhibitions as part of mutual trade-promotion efforts. This allowed American businessmen like me, who were working in Hong Kong at the time, new opportunities to reach into China.

It was decided that the first U.S. National Trade and Economic exhibition would be held in Beijing in November 1980. Many U.S. companies welcomed the idea of promoting their wares in such a potentially big new market, but were upset that the duration of the show was set at an extraordinarily long twelve days, and even more upset that the dates spanned the Thanksgiving holiday.

The dates, like myriad other details concerning the show, were subject to complex, first-time bilateral negotiations between the organizers—the China Council for Promotion of International Trade (CCPIT) and the U.S. Department of Commerce (USDOC). Among other things, CCPIT dictated which industrial sectors should be included among the exhibits. Consumer goods were excluded because attracting Chinese people to buy them was seen as a threat to China's precious reserves of foreign exchange.

The show was held in an old Soviet-style exhibition hall next to the Beijing zoo. Huge crowds began lining up before the ribbon cutting. A large sign at the entrance proclaimed the importance of "Independence and Self-Reliance," as if to exhort visitors to the show to look at the goods on display but be wary of getting swept off their feet.

About two hundred American companies were represented, including many Fortune 500 giants as well as some midsize makers of industrial products. There were literally many tons of corporate brochures printed in Chinese, as well as logo-embellished give-away items like pins, hats, bags, and keychains, as we Americans geared up for our first big marketing splash in China. Care had to be exercised in distributing color leaflets to avoid crowd control problems.

One of the exhibitors, Westinghouse, was best known for its power generation equipment and technology; but their Linguaphone subsidiary was also represented in their booth. Linguaphone produces language-study products. One afternoon a rumor swept the crowded exhibit hall that English study tapes were available for sale, in local Chinese currency, at the Westinghouse booth. The exuberant crowd that came rushing in caused the Westinghouse booth to collapse. Fortunately, no one was hurt.

The CCPIT summoned Westinghouse executives and senior US-DOC officials to criticize them sharply for overexciting the Chinese people and causing a dangerous situation. USDOC was told to warn other exhibitors not to repeat such mistakes.

As far as I could see, no one from Westinghouse had willfully triggered the stampede. Who started the rumor was a mystery and has remained so ever since. The proclamation about self-reliance at the front door stated a fundamental and well-known Chinese policy that was at least a decade old. Following a long stretch of self-imposed isolation, opening the door even a crack was a sudden departure from the stance of extreme "independence and self-reliance." It didn't take much to trigger powerful reactions among ordinary Chinese people, long hungry for a higher standard of living and more openness. It was a harbinger of the craze to learn English that was about to sweep China and would continue gaining momentum for decades to come.

For Chinese officials, it was convenient to blame foreigners. After all, if the foreigners hadn't been present, no stampede would have taken place. At a deeper level, of course, the small incident reflects the magnitude of the challenge of managing the transition from a completely closed society to a selectively open one.

悟

THE STUPIDEST THING I DID IN CHINA

Suzanne Cahill

1980

During December of 1980, in the middle of a cold, dry, and colorless Beijing winter, an American friend and I, both of us homesick, decided to cheer ourselves up by throwing a party on Christmas Eve. We planned the event for Building 25, the foreign women's dormitory at Peking University, where we lived, and invited our foreign and Chinese classmates and other expats—pretty much everyone we knew—for a night of drinking and dancing.

We decided that we needed a Christmas tree to enliven the gray cement corridor on the second floor where the festivities would take place. We managed to borrow a saw. Then we located a small pine tree inside an unguarded part of the high cement wall surrounding People's University, at that time, a closed campus that foreigners were forbidden to enter. A few nights before the party, we climbed over the wall, sawed down the tree, and managed to drag it back over the wall and into our dorm without being detected. We installed it in a bucket filled with gravel and water. Over the next few days, everyone in our dorm and in Building 26, the foreign men's dorm, contributed whatever decorations we could fashion or repurpose to make that scruffy little tree as bright and gaudy as possible.

The party was a great success, massively well attended, and as lively as we'd hoped. Several romances began that evening, and people talked about the party for months afterward. No university officials ever asked where we obtained the tree.

I told this story to my son when he was about twenty as an example of his mother's youthful folly.

EXPATS

Stephen R. MacKinnon

1979–1981

During our stay in China as "foreign experts," my wife Janice and I were thrust into the middle of the famously secretive, closeted community of Western "old friends" of the Chinese revolution, whose job descriptions were also "foreign expert." Most were couples, and most had been living as political exiles in the PRC since the 1950s.

We owed our access to this group to a great lady, the American journalist and political activist Agnes Smedley (1892–1950), whose biography we were in the midst of researching and writing. The Chinese government and, especially, Smedley's old friends in Beijing and Shanghai were eager to help.

Sol and Pat Adler and Frank and Ruth Coe were our first ushers into this rarefied world. Coe and Adler had been high-level officials in the U.S. Treasury Department under Franklin Roosevelt. Coe had been an architect of the Bretton Woods agreement. The McCarthyite witch hunts of the 1950s had forced both men into political exile. The two couples lived in the faded elegance of large courtyard compounds that were provided to them by the government's International Liaison Office. The Coe courtyard was near the Gulou drum tower in north-central Beijing, and the Adler one was farther west, not far from the zoo. The families had furnished their homes with exquisite antique Chinese furniture, and, in the case of the Adlers, a collection of very fine paintings that they had acquired during the Cultural Revolution and earlier. The Adlers originally had been advised on what to collect by Ji Chaoding, the banker extraordinaire for both Chiang Kai-shek and Mao Zedong. In the 1920s, Ji had been Frank Coe's roommate at the University of Chicago. Ji died in 1963. The Adlers' next adviser on antiques was the infamous security chief, or Mao's Rasputin, Kang Sheng. Kang was also an ardent collector and, Adler told me, occasionally invited the two couples over for tea in the 1960s. In 2016, at an auction sale of the estate of the recently deceased Pat Adler, what little remained of the fabulous Adler collection sold for millions of yuan.

Adler and Coe and their families had been protected during the Cultural Revolution by Zhou Enlai as high-level "old friends." Others in this category included Joan Hinton and Fred Engst, who lived outside of town at the Red Star Dairy. Before coming to China, Joan had been a young nuclear physicist who worked at Los Alamos on the atomic bomb. Ardent Maoists to their dying days, Joan and Fred were still angry in the late 1970s about being forced to move from the dairy into the city to live in a hotel from 1966 to 1969. But hotel life was not typical of the Cultural Revolution experience of most people in that hardy band of "old friends."

As fellow "experts," we were privileged to mingle with a number of them. We vacationed with them at Beidaihe, worked together at the *People's Daily* and the Xinhua News Agency, went on special trips, and generally socialized. We could get a feel for the texture of their community. Most had been embroiled in personal and political struggles. Khrushchev's denunciation of Stalin in 1956 had led to some mutual recriminations. Splits had led to confrontations and arrests during the Cultural Revolution, and bitterness still lingered in the late 1970s. Certain people were not speaking to certain other people. I thought the atmosphere at the Foreign Languages Press was especially poisonous. The German Ruth Weis, for example, had become something of a pariah. Central to what happened during the Cultural Revolution to this community of old lefties was Sidney Rittenberg, who became quite close to the infamous Gang of Four. The prevailing view at the time was that he had led others—like Israel Epstein, Elsie Cholmeley, Li Lisan's Russian wife, Lisa Kishkina (1914–2015), David and Isabel Crook, and others—terribly astray. They all ended up in prison. Rittenberg himself was imprisoned and not released until after Zhou Enlai's death in 1976. I recommend David and Nancy Milton's fine memoir, *The Wind Will Not Subside*, on the Maoist struggles among the "old friends" during the Cultural Revolution.

To Janice and me at the time, two figures who seemed the most noble, in part because they had suffered so greatly, were Xianyi and Gladys Yang at the Foreign Languages Press. Almost nightly the couple held salons in their apartment for Chinese intellectuals and assorted Westerners who were in residence or passing through. The price of attendance was a bottle of whiskey or good European wine. The Yangs and their guests were a great source of gossip and delicious jokes about the precarious state of the newly opening intellectual worlds of Beijing.

We also saw a great deal of Rewi Alley—the New Zealander housed in an old mansion in a compound that once housed the Italian Embassy and that was taken over in the late 1970s by the People's Friendship Association. At our first meeting, Rewi expressed much alarm about the degradation of New China's physical environment. I remember well how, on a trip to Baotou, Inner Mongolia, in 1985, he raged at our Chinese hosts on the subject of the deterioration of the Mongolian grasslands. Today Beijing is paying a huge price in terms of air pollution, just as Alley had predicted. Yet in print, he remained a loyal propagandist, always following the Party line in voluminous writings and never expressing his environmental outrage publicly, as far as I know. The same was true of Bill Hinton, author of *Fanshen* and other books.

It is not well appreciated that these old foreign friends were actually a diverse group. The most visible were the "fellow traveler" types like Alley and Epstein. But more numerous were women like Jane Su, who were married to Chinese officials, high and low, and lived in Chinese work units that were normally barred to foreigners—only to appear unexpectedly on an occasion like a birthday party.

Some figures, like Bob Winter (1887–1986), were unique. Bob had been teaching Shakespeare in Beijing since the 1920s. He was a living relic from the Bohemian expat days of Beijing in the 1920s and was still there in the 1970s. When we saw him in the late 1970s, he was already over ninety years old and a reclusive figure whom you might see riding his bicycle around the Peking University campus or taking a dip in Kunming Lake at the Summer Palace. His former students loved him, but few people really knew him. Even not knowing him, though, it could be useful to pretend that one did. In those days, entry into the walled work units where everybody lived required registering with guards. Especially at Peking University, this could be difficult. One trick that worked was to ride a bike confidently up to the gate and announce (and then register in writing) that you were visiting Bob Winter—almost the only name of a foreigner that a guard might know. For me, at least, this always worked magically, and the gates opened every time. Thank you, Bob Winter.

悟

REPRESENTATIVE OF THE BOURGEOISIE

Charlotte Furth

1981

I delivered lectures on colonial America twice a week during the 1981 fall semester at Peking University. I had been trained in Chinese history, not U.S. history, so before I set out for China, I had sought advice on textbooks and readings from American history specialists. Social history "from below" was an exciting new field at the time, and I found Gary Nash's popular monograph *Black, White, and Red*, which emphasized class, racial, and ethnic cleavages during the colonial era, to be an appealing text. I began my lectures by highlighting the relations between native American "Indians" and the white settlers, and then turned to the rapid transformations of the social landscape that slavery caused.

One might assume that this left-leaning approach would have been readily accepted within China's communist society, so I was at first a bit puzzled by the polite silence that I received from my students. I waited in office hours for feedback, but no one came.

After about three weeks, a group of three young men showed up. They had been following my lectures well enough to offer some criticism. Their spokesperson, Xu, was a good-looking, well-built young man with a natural self-confidence that in the United States would have marked him as a student leader.

"Here in China we are familiar with the Marxist interpretation of American history," he said. "What we want from you is the bourgeois version." Then, to soften the sting, all three began to compliment me on my lectures. "You pronounce all your consonants," they said, and shook their heads over the troubles they had had listening to American southerners and Australians.

Of course, I answered by saying there is no one "bourgeois version" of American history. They regarded this claim with polite incomprehension. But in fact this was an "Aha!" moment for me. I could sense that Xu and his companions were not speaking for themselves so much as representing a consensus of their peers. Now, at last, I was getting a coherent response to my lectures, and it was one that gave me a real clue about the nature of my students. They were, to use a Maoist term, young "bourgeois intellectuals"! They expected me, who came from the industrially and politically advanced United States, to profess mainstream "bourgeois" values and a story of American progress that was uncontaminated by reflections on its imperfections. Seeking to oblige, I switched from the West Coast radical Gary Nash to Harvard University's A-team—Bernard Bailyn, David Brion Davis, and their colleagues—who had produced *The Great Republic: A History of the American People* that was used in hundreds of U.S. classrooms. My lectures turned to enlightenment ideology, the British parliamentary model, constitutionalism, and states' rights, and from then on were well received. Eventually, the students were able to come up with their own critical reflections on American history and society.

FAMOUS AMERICAN SPY

Suzanne Cahill

1981

In February of 1981, during the long New Year's vacation for students at Peking University, I traveled with a young male friend all over China. We went mostly by train ("hard sleeper" class) north from Beijing to Mongolia, west along the Silk Road, back to the ancient capitals and on to Shanghai, Hangzhou, and Suzhou, and then took the "East Is Red" ferry through the Yangtze gorges. We ended up in the south, traveling from one archaeological site or famous mountain to another. In Kunming, Yunnan province, army artists stationed there told us about some unusual Buddhist ruins, influenced by Southeast Asian traditions, in a medium-sized village not too far distant. Without checking whether the place was open to foreigners, we took a five-hour bus ride there and found rooms in a cheap local hotel, planning to visit the Buddhist site the next day. The village was small, and we saw no government presence. We had dinner that evening in the hotel dining room, where a charming and handsome Red Army doctor from Beijing, who told us he was sent down to take care of the local peasants' health care needs, joined us. He said he was glad to find Mandarin speakers to hang out with.

A few hours after we retired for the night—it was around 3:00 a.m.—the door to my room swung loudly open, startling me awake. The doctor had gotten the key to my room, and he proceeded to climb into my bed and embrace me. Luckily, he was not very big or strong. Terrified and angry, I shoved him off, shouted as loudly as I could, and ran to my friend's room. About an hour later, the hotel manager came along with two policemen and arrested my traveling companion and me on the grounds that it was illegal for foreigners to be in that town as it was located in a strategic region close to the Burma border. (This was true.) After they saw our Peking University identity cards and student traveling authorizations, they let us go but told us we had to leave immediately. We sat outside the rest of the night and took a bus out of town as soon as the sun rose. We never saw the Buddhist ruins.

Up to that point on our trip, when hotel managers asked us if we were "one household" (i.e., married), we had always said we were not and requested separate rooms. After that night, we told hotelkeepers that we were indeed "one household" and requested a single room with two beds.

We traveled on for another few weeks. After we returned to Beijing, I was called into the Foreign Students' Office of Peking University and criticized for having traveled to "an important military stronghold forbidden to foreigners." The local police had written a scathing letter denouncing me as "a famous American spy." The university officials told me that, fearful of my corrupting influence on other students, they had come close to expelling me. But they never mentioned the incident again.

悟

ENCOUNTERING SHANDONG

Joseph W. Esherick

1980

I graduated from Harvard as a traditional elite-school liberal, and then, in the mid-1960s, was gradually radicalized as a grad student at Berkeley, where my involvement in the anti–Vietnam War movement developed into a broader anti-imperialism, support for national liberation movements, and a general sympathy for the Chinese revolution and its socialist experiments.

After nearly a decade of teaching at the University of Oregon, I reached China for the first time in 1979 in one of the first groups of scholars sponsored by the new program of the Committee on Scholarly Communication with the People's Republic of China. There were like-minded young faculty in that group—Philip Huang, Liz Perry, Vera Schwarcz, Linda Grove—and some impressive graduate students including Gail Hershatter and Emily Honig. We saw each other during the year, and near the end of the year, met in Beijing's Friendship Hotel to try to figure out how to rewrite our modern-history lectures to reflect the China that had emerged once our rose-tinted glasses had been removed.

Whether it was disappointment, or disillusionment, or begrudging acknowledgment of the real China that we were encountering, the process did not occur overnight. The first impressions recorded in my journal included appreciations of individualistic Chinese resistance to authority in the form of bicycle riders sweeping heedlessly through red lights. I even managed approving words for watchmen who resisted opening the gate for our Shanghai sedan—then a sign of privileged status—as it carried my sick son to a local hospital. But it was not long before the inscrutable layers of state regulations that governed our every action began to darken my mood.

There was no housing for visiting scholars at Shandong University, where I was assigned for my research project, so we were placed in the Ji'nan Hotel, where the other long-term guests were a group of Romanian engineers from a truck factory with whom we shared no common language—but still managed a hard-drinking celebration of the New Year. With no television in our room, we asked to subscribe to the local newspaper, but it proved impossible to arrange a subscription for a foreigner. Norma Diamond, University of Michigan anthropologist, was also staying in the hotel, but one day when the weather was bad and I was sick, it was impossible to share her car to the university because she was working for the Foreign Languages Department and I was in History. It was also more than a little irritating when, on a trip soon after our arrival, our handlers managed to put my eleven-year-old son in a separate car so they could quiz him on his and my relation to my partner at that time.

My research was on the Boxer Uprising, and I had chosen to locate at Shandong University because of its substantial cadre of historians working on the Boxers. A major conference on the Boxers was approaching, and the department's entire modern-history section had been mobilized for Boxer projects. Several scholars had written interesting articles that I had read, but meeting them was a non-trivial enterprise. When there were meals following a conference or on a trip, the foreigners were always segregated in a special room or at least at a separate table—preferably far removed from any Chinese guests. As required at the time, I had been assigned a primary contact, an elderly professor, Xu Xudian, trained at a Christian college before 1949. Professor Xu was a kindly scholar of the old school, but with a "bad" family background (he was a relative of the warlord-era President Xu Shichang), had suffered under incessant government campaigns, and accordingly was cautious to the point of timidity and very much isolated from the collective life of the department. Any time I wished to speak to anyone else, he would have to request through the appropriate Party and foreign affairs channels for approval. One day on campus, I ran into one of the scholars who had participated in the Boxer surveys of 1959–1962. We had met once before (through the proper channels), and I suggested that we get together again to discuss our shared scholarly interests. He reacted with near terror, said that I would first have to bring this up with Professor Xu and, sweating profusely, quickly hurried off. Indeed, sweaty encounters, even in the cold Shandong winter, were a regular theme in my journal, and it was painful to see how academic discussion with a foreigner engendered so much anxiety.

As I traveled around to visit colleagues at other universities, I came to realize how much Shandong, with its toxic combination of cultural conservatism and Cultural Revolution legacies, lagged behind other provinces. The wounds of the Cultural Revolution struggles were still fresh and Party authorities were settling scores. Foreigners were not a welcome addition to the local scene, and we often found ourselves used for others' ends. One day, outside the foreign experts' dining hall, a notice was posted that because Shandong University would be hosting more foreigners, chickens and vegetable gardens would henceforth be banned from the compound. We protested that foreigners had no objection to either chickens or vegetables but succeeded only in getting foreigners removed as the excuse for the new regulation. Another protest was more successful. When a notice appeared saying that the lovely old shade trees on campus would be cut down and replaced by "new trees" (i.e., tiny saplings), we tacked notices to the trees proclaiming that foreigners love trees. Trees in our immediate area were saved, but somehow, from another part of the campus, the university fulfilled its obligation to supply lumber for the growing economy.

My research tour in Shandong focused on two objectives: perusing the records of the oral histories that the university had conducted in the 1950s and 1960s and visiting the main Boxer areas myself. It was only after five months of pleading, around the Spring Festival holidays, that I got to read the interview records, and they were wonderful and well worth the wait. Securing permission for fieldwork in the countryside was even more challenging. Regular meetings on this request produced a wide range of complications: there was no precedent; there were no hotels for foreigners; toilet facilities were not suitable; security could not be guaranteed; permission was denied by the military district; and on and on. As time grew short and my requests more insistent, the department Party secretary took over the negotiations.

Chen Zhi'an was a tall, lean, soft-spoken, well-liked, and endlessly patient Party secretary in the History Department. As was normal practice in those days, he was introduced as the deputy head of the department, and it was only after some time that I realized he was the Party secretary and the key figure in whose hands my fate lay. Over time, he gently let it be known that resistance to my fieldwork was due to my own reactionary behavior—especially my photographing "backward" aspects of China's landscape and my walking into a publicly announced trial in a provisional courtroom near the university. Apparently, I made an adequate apology and self-criticism, for finally in May, my fieldwork was approved.

Fieldwork in the summer of 1980 was the high point of that first year in China for me, but it was also a reminder of the rich variety in local interpretations of the new barbarian-management regulations. My first rural stop was memorable: a new large bed had been purchased and new sheets sewn together to fit it; a nail had been pounded into the mud wall to hold the pink toilet paper; my room still smelled of fresh paint, and both bedroom and dining room were furnished with hard candies and cigarettes—always carefully placed with *pinyin* side up. My meals were served with sugar for the rice and canned fruit for dessert. The cost was three *yuan* for the room, six *yuan* for three meals, and another three *yuan* for the hundred-kilometer car ride. At the large prefectural town of Dezhou, the room rate jumped to thirty *yuan*. In the Boxer stronghold of Chiping, I was hosted for lunch by the entire county leadership, who made a valiant effort to get me drunk enough on white-lightning liquor to prevent an afternoon interview session. (They failed, just barely, thanks to a lot of tea and my pacing about during the siesta hour.) When I got to a Boxer site now remapped onto the Hebei side of the border, the reception was notably more open, generous, and professional. Shandong was indeed a world apart.

悟

HIGH IN TIBET

Melinda Liu

1980

When Washington and Beijing normalized diplomatic ties, I was working as a journalist in Hong Kong, covering the Chinese economy for the *Far Eastern Economic Review*. My cubicle was next to that of David Bonavia, a legendary China watcher who spoke seven languages and had a wicked sense of humor. Diplomatic normalization opened the doors for American news organizations to establish news bureaus in Beijing. I left the *Review* when *Newsweek* hired me to open its bureau in Beijing, and I arrived in the Chinese capital in March 1980. I was delighted to discover David was also living in Beijing, now working with a British paper. We chatted about applying for permission to visit dozens of Chinese cities, many of which had not been accessible to independent Western reporters for years or even decades. For me, visiting Tibet was at the top of the list.

In the summer of 1980, I got my chance. I was among a dozen or more foreign correspondents chosen by the Chinese Foreign Ministry to visit Tibet. Traveling to the roof of the world was nearly as exotic for many of the Foreign Ministry handlers who accompanied us as it was for us reporters. Upon arrival at a high-altitude airport outside the city, we were herded onto a jolting rattletrap of a bus for the long ride into Lhasa. For hours we bounced along—Foreign Ministry officials, expectant foreign media, and a Chinese male translator attached to a U.S. news bureau, whose trip we journalists had bankrolled in hopes of getting an unvarnished version of events.

Arriving in Lhasa, many of us were looking green around the gills. But we didn't want to waste time "resting for the afternoon," as our handlers suggested. We demanded to begin reporting right away. The local officials who had greeted us—most of them Han Chinese—insisted this was unwise. Our Foreign Ministry handlers from Beijing tried to find a compromise, but were criticized by both sides. Tensions rose. Finally we journalists compromised by agreeing to stay in the guesthouse for a couple of hours—but on one condition. We insisted on using the time to discuss and fine-tune our itinerary and schedule, to try to ensure opportunity for as much reporting as possible.

The Lhasa-based Chinese officials were beginning to appear irritated by the demands of their stubborn and ignorant visitors. We gathered in a meeting area, sinking down into armchairs and a sofa with lace antimacassars around a low coffee table. Our unfortunate translator was looking pale. Suffering from the high altitude, he was already clutching a bag of oxygen; it looked like a large, thick-skinned balloon attached to a slender hose, one end of which was stuck into his left nostril. A few of the Foreign Ministry handlers also appeared a bit haggard.

We started discussing the schedule. We reporters demanded to see more temples, to interview more monks, and to experience more grassroots encounters instead of listening to endless briefings while sitting in plush armchairs with antimacassars. Voices rose. The poor translator struggled to keep up. He looked agitated, then began fiddling furiously with the tube stuck into his nose.

In the middle of this increasingly heated discussion, he suddenly vomited all over the coffee table. (Nausea is a common symptom of altitude sickness.) That ended the meeting. We decided perhaps it was a good idea to rest in our rooms for the remainder of the afternoon, after all.

Such was the beginning of a trip rife with cultural misunderstandings, not just between Western reporters and Chinese officialdom, but also between the Beijing-based authorities and the Lhasa-based ones. Some of the culture clashes were hilarious. In Lhasa, we were housed in one of only two guesthouses, which had (occasional) hot water. We had to sleep two to a room, because decent accommodations were scarce. David Bonavia was adamant on having a room to himself. "I'm too old to be sharing a room," he muttered to me. I responded, "Let's see how you convince the handlers to make an exception just for you."

He walked over to our Foreign Ministry colleagues, spoke with them briefly, then came back brandishing a room key, beaming. "What did you tell them?" I asked. "It was simple," he said, "I explained to them I was diabetic and needed privacy so that I could take my insulin injections. They weren't convinced by that." A familiar impish grin spread across his face, "So then I told them I was a homosexual so it would not be safe to put either a man or a woman in the room with me. They didn't know what to say or think. . . . I got a private room." The Chinese officials, still staring at David, did indeed seem dumbstruck.

In allocating Lhasa's sparse hotel space, apparently the left hand of Chinese officialdom didn't exactly know what the right hand was doing. One day we arrived back at our guesthouse to witness a great hubbub in the next-door guesthouse, where a huge crowd of Tibetan Buddhist devotees were gathered. Some were prostrating full length on the ground, many were weeping and wailing in Tibetan. A number of Tibetan men were very tall, tanned and muscular, with long braided hair festooned with jaunty red tassels and coral and turquoise ornaments. What was going on?

It turned out that the other guesthouse housed a visiting delegation of Tibetans living abroad. They'd been sent by the exiled Tibetan religious leader, the Dalai Lama, who was curious to know if Mao Zedong's death and the beginning of China's "opening up" might pave the way for his return. Deprived of contact with their religious leader for decades, ordinary Tibetans had traveled from near and far to meet this delegation.

We reporters discovered that we could talk with the Buddhist devotees and the Tibetan delegation members by clambering up on the wall between the two guesthouses and shouting questions at them. We did that until we were shooed down from the wall by our own handlers and told to stop trying to conduct unauthorized interviews. Our frazzled Foreign Ministry colleagues found themselves trying to mediate between feisty Western reporters and conservative local authorities, who appeared not to have received the memo about China's new era of openness and reform.

In Lhasa, Tibetans often greeted the foreign media warmly. They stuck out their tongues at us—a startling move, to us, but actually a traditional Tibetan greeting—and sometimes burst into laughter and song when they saw our group. We were amazed at how ancient the old city felt. It teemed with Buddhist pilgrims and even quite a number of Muslim Hui, who lived in their own quarter downtown and who told us they'd been given permission to live in Lhasa by emperor Qian Long (r. 1735–1796). Many Tibetans had endured great hardship and suffering during the 1966–1976 Cultural Revolution and were keen to rebuild a normal society. I saw remains of temples that had been shuttered, the Buddhist deities removed; in one, the central altar, which should have housed an important Buddhist icon, instead held a giant portrait of Mao.

On the evening before our scheduled departure, we were told to pack our suitcases and place them outside our hotel rooms so they could be collected and sent to the airport ahead of time. We had to be ready to depart with our hand-carried luggage by 5:00 a.m.; our exact departure time would depend on the weather. Well, that morning it rained so hard our flight was delayed—first by one day, then another. Unfortunately, our checked bags never came back from the airport. Some of us were stuck with few clean clothes and—worse, in the eyes of our hosts—time to kill in Lhasa.

We began bargaining for additional interview opportunities, for transportation around town, for Tibetan translators who could help us talk with ordinary residents. The local Lhasa-based officials at first refused and then still insisted we pay a "service fee" for things such as transport and translators even for days when we didn't have any official activities aside from waiting for planes that never arrived. "If you don't pay," warned one of the more doctrinaire Lhasa-based Chinese officials, "you won't be allowed to leave Tibet." Some of us—me, for example—thought that was just fine. We loved exploring the old medieval city, redolent with juniper incense and yak butter.

But things were getting ugly. Some reporters began privately referring to the Lhasa-based official who'd threatened us as "Mr. Gang of Four" because he seemed so rude and xenophobic. In those days, this was a gravely serious accusation. The "Gang of Four," led by Mao's widow Jiang Qing, had been toppled a few years earlier and was blamed for an endless list of murders, mayhem, and abuses of power. Being labeled a "Gang of Four element" was not just an insult but also a charge that could mean serious professional or even physical harm.

Finally, interpersonal frictions erupted. During yet another negotiation, David Bonavia shouted at the man in question, loudly accusing him of being a Gang of Four element. The Chinese guy was apoplectic. Our Foreign Ministry handlers looked aghast. We were ordered to go to our hotel rooms immediately.

Not long afterward, I heard a knock on my door. It was one of the Foreign Ministry people, ashen faced. She explained that what David had said was an extremely serious matter; then she asked if I would agree to be part of a journalists' "mediation committee" to try to help facilitate our departure from Tibet. She seemed genuinely distraught at the thought that we might never leave. Apparently, the Lhasa-based authorities had agreed to decrease the fees demanded for those extra days when no transport or translation was provided. But in return, David would have to apologize publicly to the man we had secretly dubbed Mr. Gang of Four. Perhaps knowing I was close friends with David, the Foreign Ministry official asked if I could talk with him to try to break the impasse. I said I'd try.

I knocked on David's door; he was in a good mood when he answered it. We might have consumed a few sips of whiskey as I explained the situation; David agreed to apologize without hesitation. Everyone was summoned to yet another meeting. David gallantly and proactively stepped forward immediately to say to our recalcitrant host, "I'm sorry I called you a Gang of Four element. I must have been suffering from altitude sickness." The guy was still fuming, but at least the logjam had been broken. We were told we could leave the following morning, weather permitting. The next day dawned with a brilliant blue sky, and we flew out of Tibet having stayed five days longer than we thought we would have on the roof of the world—five days of culture clashes, diplomatic drama, and insights into Chinese officialdom's not-entirely-smooth transition from Maoist ideology into a new era of "opening up." To this day, it remains one of my favorite reporting trips.

Part IV

悟

Where Are We Going?

Despite intermittent crackdowns on "bourgeois liberalism" (1981) and "spiritual pollution" (1983), the post-Mao liberalization of Chinese society on the whole continued through the early 1980s in response to pressure from a populace that kept pushing for it. By 1985 the "reform" trend had reached an apex, and "opening" to the world went forward as well. For Westerners, the avenues to get into China and to work there became more numerous, and the required permissions became more routine. Foreigners' assignments of location and official status were still controlled by Chinese government offices, but everyday Chinese life churned along as always, and, as the essays in this section show, Westerners often—in some cases very quickly—encountered it and even became immersed in it.

悟

MY FATHER'S HOMETOWN

Mayfair Yang

1982

During the Chinese New Year holidays in February 1982, my husband, Eric, and I took the train from Beijing to visit my father's rela-

61

tives in Jiangxi province. My personal experiences with my father's family turned out to be a rich supplement to my field research as a professional anthropologist carried out elsewhere in China.

We went first to the city of Fuzhou, south of Nanchang, to visit my aunt. At the door to her apartment, we stopped dead in our tracks, confronted with the gruesome sight of a woman sitting on a low stool, using a large pair of scissors to snip off the heads of a mound of live frogs. She was my first cousin, preparing our lunch! My aunt and uncle greeted us warmly, and introduced us to my grandmother, a small, frail, bony woman. She was hunched over with osteoporosis that had bent her neck so much that her lowered head was almost at a right angle to her torso. Almost ninety years old, my grandmother was puzzled by my not understanding her Jiangxi language. She thought that I was hard of hearing and kept on cupping her hands to my ear and yelling into it repeatedly. She showed me her two thumbs, which were permanently bent at right angles. During the Cultural Revolution, when she was already in her mid-seventies, Red Guards broke into her home, strung her whole body up by her two thumbs on the roof rafter beam, and beat her, breaking her thumbs.

Just then, a rooster walked right into the apartment, my grandmother spit on the floor, and the rooster bent down to pick at the spittle. My cousin served us each a large bowl of sweet soup with eight cooked eggs floating in it and repeatedly urged us to eat it all down. We were overwhelmed with such generosity and did our best to dutifully swallow as many eggs as possible, only to later realize that their urging was part of the exaggerated hospitality of Chinese culture, and we were not actually supposed to consume all of it. Next, we had to resolutely confront the deep-fried frogs for lunch.

From Fuzhou, we got into a car sent by the county government to ferry us up a long winding mountain road to my father's hometown in the Wuyi Mountains of Jiangxi. We had to make some adjustments when we arrived because we had never seen such poverty. The town had a medieval feeling about it, with very few cars. The streets were densely packed with people, some with shoulder poles loaded with produce or grain. The whole area was closely tied in with agriculture; there were stores selling agricultural tools such as plows, rakes, and fertilizer, or servicing agricultural machinery. Most of the buildings, which dated to the 1930s and 1940s, were decrepit two-story traditional wooden row houses where the downstairs served as small shops or restaurants, and people slept upstairs. These buildings were on their last legs, but they were still bursting with human residents. Here and there on the streets, we saw middle-aged women and men with bald patches on their head, a mark of earlier years of malnutrition, and many had bad teeth. When my husband went to a public bathhouse to take a shower with my male relatives, he later reported how shocked he was seeing their thin and frail bodies with their ribcages prominently displayed. It was winter and people wore cotton-padded jackets that were faded and patched. It was also around Chinese New Year, so families were celebrating by buying and eating meat and fish that they could not normally afford. We saw a lot of salted meat and fish hanging from almost every building, drying in the sun, to be stored and eaten gradually over the rest of the year.

Old and faded Cultural Revolution slogans still covered the sides of many brick buildings and walls, such as "Our Whole Hearts are Thinking about Chairman Mao; All that we do is for Chairman Mao!" (一心想着毛主席; 一切为了毛主席) and "In Agriculture, Learn from Dazhai!" (农业学大寨!). On the side of one building, I was amazed to see, showing beneath a Cultural Revolution slogan, the faded yet still discernible slogan of the Guomindang era, "Three Principles of the People" (三民主義). Suddenly, I was seized with the thought that places such as this in China were poor because so many destructive historical forces had swept through, one after another. First, the Taiping Rebellion's rebel army (1850–1864) fought with Qing imperial troops here, resulting in the decimation of about a third of the population. Next, Japanese troops invaded and killed people, narrowly missing my father, who was standing next to a tree that got hit by a Japanese bomb. Then the Communist guerrillas holed up in Jiangxi, one of the poorer provinces, and fought against the Guomindang here in the Civil War. The famine caused by the disastrous Great Leap Forward killed off people here in the untold hundreds of thousands. The latest scourge was the Cultural Revolution, with more people succumbing to persecution, suicide, or factional fighting. Each time, as the residents recovered from a previous disaster and tried to get back on their feet, they were soon knocked down by the next man-made scourge.

The only delightful part of the town's landscape was the six-hundred-year-old painted wooden bridge that dated back to the Ming Dynasty. It spanned a deep ravine and a mountain stream below. This bridge was such a rare treasure, with benches built into its sides and paintings of late imperial gentlemen and ladies enjoying leisure activities in their gentry homes. People liked to linger on the bridge, smoking, chatting, and listening to music on someone's radio or cassette player or to the rushing waters beneath, especially at dusk and in the evenings. I worried about the heavy smoking and how people carelessly stubbed out their cigarette butts directly on the precious wood. So it was with great pain and regret that in 2006, when I returned to attend my father's funeral in this town, I learned that the beautiful bridge had burned down and had been replaced by a modern cement bridge.

This town was so isolated in the mountains, and so few of its people had ever left the local area, that my husband, a British American with a beard, became a star attraction. It was clear that for everyone in the town, this was their first time seeing a Westerner in the flesh. Whenever we went out on the streets, a crowd of hundreds of people would gather to gawk, and a few brave ones close to Eric would reach out their hand to stroke his beard and hair-covered arms. There were looks of awe, delight, horror, even disgust. I saw people on bicycles stop and get off their bikes, and quite a few riding past, turn their heads back to gaze. One poor fellow's eyes were so glued to my husband's head rising above the crowd that he rode into a telephone pole and fell off his bike! Others bumped into each other and started to quarrel about who was at fault. A woman raised her toddler onto her shoulders to see the foreigner, warning him, "Next time you misbehave, I will feed you to him!" The child's face broke up and he cried out in fear. The crowds got bigger and traffic snarled until, finally, the local authorities requested that we avoid going out except in a car.

We were lodged in the small dormitory of the county government headquarters. When we first visited my Second Uncle's home, we were in for a shock. His family of eight people (he had six children) were all jammed into a single room of the old Yang family mansion, built sometime in the Qing Dynasty. The rest of the now broken-down mansion had been divided up among poor peasant families, and one part had been made into a rice granary and husking mill owned by the county government. Thus, the old family mansion was full of unrelated people living cheek by jowl, with chickens and kids running around the little courtyards that opened up to the sky, and different families cooking their meals in makeshift tiny kitchens and doing their laundry on washboards in large wooden basins. Inside my uncle's room was a giant round vat that was as high as my thighs, about four feet in circumference, with a large round wooden lid covering it. I found out the purpose of the vat when I asked to go to the bathroom.

I was led up the small steps on the side of the vat, they lifted up the giant lid, and an atrocious odor permeated the room. It was a giant vat of night soil, and by sticking out my butt over the edge of the vat, I was going to make one more contribution to the storage of human fertilizer for the fields!

The next time I visited that room, I asked to go to a different type of toilet, so they took me to the public toilet of a county government office nearby. Inside were rows of rectangular holes, and I squatted down over a hole in a stall and held my nose from the bad odor as I went about my business. Suddenly, I noticed a movement and scurrying sound down below. Alarmed, I looked down, thinking a human Peeping Tom was down there. Squinting into the dark below, I saw a giant rat almost the size of a small cat, holding something in his paws, eating and chewing away. I ran out of the public toilet, in horror and disgust, and told my aunt what I had seen. "Yes," she nodded matter-of-factly, "here the rats do eat human shit." I had never seen such large rats, and my aunt explained that this area attracted them because of the rice granary next door. "Check it out over there, you'll find them there," she told me. Sure enough, when Eric and I ventured over to the granary, we saw several large ones. One even approached our feet and, showing no fear at all, boldly looked up at us. We bolted out of there like a streak of lightning.

We went to a hospital to visit my middle-aged cousin, son of my father's older sister who had died before the Communist revolution. The hospital also presented a big shock to us. Upon first entering the grounds, we heard the distant heartrending cries of dogs in pain. We later found out that those dogs were probably subjects of medical experiments being carried out. We were astounded that there seemed to be no effort to keep such experimentation out of earshot, and the other denizens of the hospital seemed to treat the cries as normal. My cousin was in the hospital trying to recover from the severe case of tuberculosis that he had contracted in prison. He had been thrown into prison during the Cultural Revolution for a terrible mistake he made. Since he was good at painting portraits, some Red Guards drafted him into an effort to produce portraits of Chairman Mao for mounting on walls. My cousin was not thinking when he painted a black frame around a portrait of Mao. He was accused of wishing for the death of Chairman Mao, and no amount of his denial was sufficient to save him. He was thrown into prison for his political mistake. When we visited him, his appearance was ghastly. He was bone thin, and his body was filthy.

Evidently they did not bother to bathe him in the hospital. He made a valiant effort to seem cheerful and carefree, but I was not surprised to learn a few months later that he had passed away.

悟

HIGH-RISE COUNTERCULTURE

Paul G. Pickowicz

1982

In fall 1982, I was living in Beijing carrying on research at the Film Archive of China. I was on an exchange program administered by the Committee on Scholarly Exchange with the PRC and was the first U.S. China scholar to gain long-term research access to the mysterious archive. Virtually all films made from 1922 to 1966 had been denounced and banned during Mao's Cultural Revolution, but by the early 1980s, some officials in the vast Chinese cultural bureaucracy felt that it was time to reconsider this harsh verdict and were eager to have foreign scholars weigh in.

One of my best friends in those days was a young Manchu guy. This was still very much a time when foreigners living in China were not supposed to have private friends. I met him through the good graces of a Western journalist with whom he was friendly. I liked spending time with him in large part because he seemed to circulate in a subculture that was out of sight and out of bounds for foreigners. He had his own bachelor pad in one of the many grim Stalinist-type residential high-rise buildings in the Sanlihe neighborhood. He used a huge Chinese flag as a bedspread. He had a motorcycle complete with sidecar—a Harley-Davidson knockoff marketed under the brand name Liberation.

There was virtually no public-space nightlife in Beijing in those days. Young people made their own private-space plans. One Friday night in late fall, my friend said, "Let's go out. I want you to meet some friends of mine. . . . By the way," he added, "bring along some of your audio tapes." We went by motorcycle to an ugly apartment complex. There was no elevator in the building we entered, the stairwell was completely dark, and a large number of bicycles were crammed inside on the ground floor. We made our way past the bikes, went up several floors, and knocked on an apartment door. A young woman and her husband let us in, and we saw at once that several others were already gathered in the surprisingly large sitting room.

"What's this?" I asked my friend.

"A dance party," he mumbled. Now I knew why he wanted me to bring my Bee Gees tapes.

As introductions were being made, I noticed a steady stream of new arrivals. Of special note were young, working-class women, still dressed in their bland, unisex work clothes, each carrying a bulky parcel. The women disappeared into a back room, only to reappear one by one twenty minutes later in an entirely different outfit. Some of them wore the type of glamorous, high-collared *qipao* gown favored by stylish Shanghai women in the 1920s and 1930s. They had also applied tasteful makeup and sported attractive hairstyles. They knew how to dress in such clothing. They looked beautiful and attractive in an understated kind of way. But I had never seen anyone dressed like this in public. How had they mastered the "look," and why did they like it?

Our host told me that this group of friends often met on weekends for dance parties of this sort. He said they always informed their neighbors that there would be more than the usual amount of noise. They also put blankets up to cover all the windows so that the interior lights would not be apparent to nosy passersby late at night.

Before long, a boom box was produced and the music began. My audio tapes were especially welcomed because they were first generation, not the usual sort of inferior tapes that had been copied multiple times. When the dancing began, I could not help but notice that the quality of dancing was very good. Not only did people look nice, but they knew how to dance and were clearly enjoying themselves enormously. Word began to circulate that I was an American. A couple of the young women came over and asked me to dance.

"You are an American," the first one said, "so you can dance very well!" Unfortunately, my moves did not amount to very much, and the women were bitterly disappointed. "Are you sure he's an American?"

Still, everyone had great fun, all the way until three or four in the morning. Then, one by one, the women retreated to the back room, removed the makeup, removed the gorgeous clothing, readjusted hairstyles, and reappeared in their work clothes before saying good-bye and heading for the early morning streets. In their heart of hearts, I wondered, what were these young people really like? More like their public-space personas or more like their private-space personas?

SECOND UNCLE AND HIS WIFE

Mayfair Yang

1982

My father was the oldest son in a former landlord's family, in a rural mountain town in Jiangxi, with two other sons and two daughters. My father's second brother, whom I called Second Uncle, was a thin wiry man in his fifties. He was the head of an eight-member family who were all squeezed into just one room of the family's now decrepit mansion after the other rooms were given out to peasants. Unlike my father and Third Uncle (the youngest son), who both left the Mainland for Taiwan in 1949, Second Uncle had stayed in the hometown during the Civil War. I learned that in the 1940s, when my father was away studying in Chongqing, Guomindang troops came to their town to draft more troops for their depleted forces. They demanded that every family provide one adult son to join their military forces. My father's family decided that since their youngest son, my Third Uncle, was too young, Second Uncle should join the Guomindang. But Second Uncle adamantly refused, so Third Uncle was drafted instead. At the young age of eighteen, he fought a brutal battle against Communist troops on Guning Island as he accompanied the Guomindang in their retreat to Taiwan.

Second Uncle's refusal to join the Guomindang proved to be a fateful decision because after the Communists took over China, he suffered a great deal by staying in the mountain town. As the son of a landlord, he and his family were treated as outcasts. They lived a life of poverty and political harassment. During the Cultural Revolution, Second Uncle was beaten and thrown into a labor camp. Things got worse when people found out they had relatives in Taiwan. Meanwhile, in Taiwan, Third Uncle avoided all the suffering meted out to those of bad birth in Maoist society. Third Uncle rose in the military ranks, married a local Taiwanese woman, had three children, enjoyed a comfortable life in Taiwan, and eventually emigrated to the United States. Such are the unpredictable twists and turns of personal fortunes in history.

During our stay in the impoverished town, Second Uncle and his family treated my husband and me to a banquet. Since a Western foreigner was visiting, his family had been given food coupons to go into the special stores that normally are open only to the local officials. With these coupons, they could purchase the strong maotai liquor that was a luxury good difficult for most Chinese to acquire. They also could buy scarce food items such as pork and chicken to entertain us. Pork fat was an important ingredient. The "red-cooked pork" dish was made up of chunks of pork with alternating layers of fat and lean meat. There was even a dish of deep-fried pork fat, rolled in sugar. I could understand the local love of fat, because so many Chinese craved it after the lean Three Years of Hardship (1959–1961), when there was a nationwide famine and people rarely tasted meat, and lard was rarely available to fry their vegetables. It was just difficult for us to eat so much fat.

During the chaotic days of the Cultural Revolution, Second Uncle joined a Red Guard faction composed mainly of people who came from bad class backgrounds. He described how he personally witnessed carnage on the streets of his town. A rival Red Guard faction had gotten hold of a military tank from a nearby army depot. The youths who climbed into the tank did not know how to operate it, and as they approached my uncle's faction down the street, the tank wobbled left and right down the street toward them. Suddenly, the main gun turret of the tank started to rise up, and everyone in my uncle's group scattered to the four winds, taking that as a sign that their enemies were going to fire. However, before the gun could fire, the controller clumsily swung the gun around in the opposite direction, so that he fired backward, upon his own Red Guard mates who had been following behind the tank! Second Uncle recalled the bloody scene as the opposing faction screamed with horror at the disaster created by friendly fire and scurried around to pick up their dead and wounded on the street.

I never learned why Second Uncle was thrown into a labor camp, but his wife took me aside and poured out her tales of woe and suffering while her husband was locked up. For several years, she had to feed and clothe the children all by herself. She labored day and night to make enough money. It did not help that Second Uncle and his wife had six children. She cried bitterly in retelling her miseries and hardships. She would occasionally save her own food so that she could bring food to her husband during her visits with him. Three of their sons developed a form of muscular dystrophy, and eventually all three lost their ability to walk. Before he was unable to walk, one of these sons managed to study at Wuhan University, received a degree in sociology, and became a scholar. He was later confined to a wheelchair and had to work from home. When my father visited his family in 1985, he bought a small building that he made into a sort of Yang Family ancestor hall, named it "Hall of Longing for Kin," and installed an altar to present incense in front of photos of his mother and father. Two of my Second Uncle's handicapped sons were able to use the ground floor as a shop fronting the street. They made it an electric-appliance repair shop that enabled them to be financially self-reliant, until both passed away.

MANUSCRIPT

Stanley Rosen

1982

In 1982, on my fourth trip to China and my second trip as an individual traveler, I felt comfortable booking my own accommodations. A political scientist from the University of Southern California, I had always had interests in popular culture, so wanted to live in a modest place outside of tourist circles. I checked first with the local Beijing travel office where foreigners could find out which hotels were permissible for foreigner travelers. I settled on a hotel run by a rural production brigade in the far south of Beijing, near the old Yongdingmen Railway Station. The station had been in use from 1897 to 2006 and was replaced when the Beijing South Railway Station opened in 2008. It was located in the Fengtai District of Beijing, 4.7 miles south of central Beijing. Despite the distance, I was attracted to the hotel since it was the cheapest place (eight *yuan* a night for a cot in a room with many others) that I could find, and I would get an opportunity to experience a section of Beijing with which I was unfamiliar.

Almost all the residents appeared to be European backpackers and, being in a relatively isolated location with little to do at night, I amused myself by sitting next to the front desk and watching and listening to the hotel guests—who almost uniformly spoke no Chinese— trying to make themselves understood by the hotel staff, who spoke no European languages. To my credit, I did try to be helpful when I could, by interpreting, although, less laudable, I usually waited until there was considerable exasperation on both sides.

One night, while I was doing this, a middle-aged Chinese man sat down next to me and said that he had heard me speaking Chinese and wanted me to meet him at the White Pagoda in Beihai Park early the next morning. I asked him what it was about, but all he would say was that it was "political." Intrigued, I told him that I would never be able to get up that early, so we agreed to meet at 11:00 a.m. Because bus service from that far south was not as convenient as I had expected, I didn't arrive at the designated location until 11:30. The gentleman was nowhere to be seen.

I forgot about the matter, but on my last evening in Beijing, the same fellow showed up in front of my hotel and told me that he had waited until 11:15 that morning but, with so many people around, he had gotten nervous and left.

It turned out that the political issue on which he wanted my help related to problems in Hangzhou, in distant Zhejiang province, that dated back to the Cultural Revolution. He had been a teacher in a high school, and when the Cultural Revolution began, he became involved with one of the factions and had taken part in denouncing the school leadership. After the Cultural Revolution, when the overthrown "power holders" were exonerated and given their old jobs back, he was dismissed and had been trying ever since to get rehired. He had exhausted all the usual petitioning channels and had become desperate, incorporating the details of his case into a long manuscript, which he pulled out and put in my hands. He asked me to take the manuscript to the *New York Times,* or another Western outlet, which he felt would compel the local authorities to restore him to his old position. Looking at the manuscript, I noticed that he was very specific in naming those who he felt had wronged him.

I told him that I didn't think Western newspapers would necessarily be interested in his case and suggested perhaps some Hong Kong magazine such as *Zhengming*, which published sensitive information that could not be published in China, but he didn't trust a Hong Kong publication and, in any case, was convinced that only a reputable Western source would be able to influence Chinese authorities. I also tried to explain to him that if I tried to carry such an explosive manuscript outside China and was caught with it, it would go very badly for him, and that he therefore probably should not take that risk. In the end, we parted, and he went looking for another Chinese-speaking foreigner who might be more helpful, or at least have more courage.

THE LOCAL OFFICIALS:
WHIFFS OF THE QING DYNASTY

Mayfair Yang

1982

The lengthiest contact my husband and I had with the local officials in my father's ancestral rural town in Jiangxi was at a banquet to which they invited us, together with my local relatives. Oddly, these powerful officials seemed just as nervous and ill at ease as our relatives and us. I suppose they were nervous about how to deal with an overseas Chinese and a Westerner, a situation that was new to them. They may also have been anxious about being placed in an awkward situation where they had to balance two very different sets of people. On the one hand, they were used to having power over my relatives, who were of low status and who greatly feared them. On the other, my husband and I were honored guests from abroad who had to be treated with respect and care. Our presence and association with my relatives empowered my relatives to a certain extent, making it difficult for the officials to maintain a consistent attitude toward them. This awkward and ambiguous set of shifting power relations vividly played out during the banquet.

My relatives regarded these officials with a combination of fear and hatred. Before the banquet, my cousin told me that he had learned over the years how to deal with officials. If one has the fortune to sit down as equals at a banquet with them, one must make them drink as much as possible. That way, they will become drunk, their power will be neutralized, and they may even lose control and embarrass themselves. He showed me a trick he had developed about how to press others to drink and to pretend to drink himself but to avoid getting drunk. He pulled out a cloth handkerchief hidden under one of his long sleeves and demonstrated how to spit his alcohol into the handkerchief, then slip the handkerchief back out of sight into his sleeve. The method allowed him to drink many times without inebriation while justifiably pressuring the officials to keep up with him. Sure enough, my cousin stood up a few times during the banquet to engage in the agonistic ritual of prodding the officials to drink more. At one point during the banquet, Second Uncle leaned over to me and whispered in my ear, "You see that fat official across the table? He was in charge of the labor camp that I was sent to for so many years! He was once so above me, he had such absolute power over everyone in the camp! He terrorized us. Now, after all these years, I am sitting across the table from him, eating with him like an equal!" As he spoke these words, I felt a spine-chilling tingle down my back, as if I had been transported back to the dreaded labor camp with my uncle. I could clearly see that there was no love lost between ordinary people like my relatives and these all-powerful officials, one of whom was unusually plump, while nearly everyone else in the area was so thin.

In Beijing, we had been invited to many impressive banquets. However, I soon realized to my great discomfort that this banquet in this impoverished small town was the most delicious and lavish banquet we had yet experienced in China. There were luxury foods such as turtle, shark fins, and bird's nest soup. There were several kinds of fish, poultry, and meat, including beef, which at that time was not common in China. There were so many different dishes that we lost count, and the final two dishes arrived when everyone had stuffed themselves so much that the dishes were left untouched. Of all places, it felt really strange to be eating so well amid such malnourishment.

A few days after the banquet with the officials, as we were preparing to depart the town, my relatives wanted to speak with us. They had purchased a large framed Chinese painting and gotten a calligrapher to write on it some words of dedication and thanks to the local officials. My relatives instructed us to take this painting to the county government's office and present it humbly to the officials, in thanks for hosting us at the banquet and for their hospitality on our visit. They wanted us to practice the little ritual we would conduct in this gift-giving ceremony. They kept pressing our heads down with their hands in respectful bows toward the officials. I was a bit annoyed, and retorted, "Why do we need to 'nod our heads and bow our waists' (點頭哈腰) towards them? We come from abroad and should not need to do this sort of thing!" They responded that if we did not humiliate ourselves in this way, after we left town, they would end up suffering at the hands of the vengeful officials. So we acquiesced and did our best to fawn over the officials with great humility.

As we drove down the winding mountain road to the Jiangxi plains, I felt as if we were leaving late imperial China and returning to the present. Up there, we were caught in a time warp where the common people regarded officials with fear, and felt obliged to bow and scrape to them, just as people did toward imperial officials in the Ming and Qing Dynasties. Somehow, in this remote corner of China, a revolution had not made much of a dent in changing the long-standing fraught relationship between officials and the common people.

悟

A FITTING CHAIR

Jennifer Anderson

1983

In 1982, after two years as a student of modern Chinese literature at Nanjing University, I returned to Melbourne, Australia, to complete a Diploma of Education. Upon graduation I was offered a one-year fellowship to go back to Nanjing, this time as a teacher-scholar under a sister-province relationship between Jiangsu and Victoria.

Hence it happened that, in February 1983, I found myself again a resident in a foreign-student dormitory at Nanjing University. This time, though, my status was different. My assigned room was not a regular student room but one on the ground floor, which was reserved for short-term researchers or teachers. I made myself comfortable in it and began my teaching of English conversation classes at the Normal College just down the road.

About six weeks later, I came back to my room to find a sofa chair in its center. The chair had the same impressive girth and large padded arms as those I'd seen in the rooms of professors and higher-level officials. It was covered in apricot brocade that was now rather grubby and worse for wear; and one of its arms had been wrenched away from the seat frame.

At first I was disappointed at its tawdry condition but later realized—and was amused—that the sofa chair suited me perfectly. I was not a professor or a middle-rank official. I was a *zhuanjia* (expert), but not an experienced one, and had only the equivalent of a bachelor's degree. In my imagination, I saw the comrades in the Foreign Affairs office discussing my status and then searching high and low for a chair to match.

I remembered that one of the key Confucian precepts, known in English as the Rectification of Names, emphasized the notion that harmony is achieved when all people perform their prescribed roles properly. I had seen these roles given delineation in the cut and fabric of a Sun Yatsen suit, in the quality of footwear, or in the brand of cigarettes one used. Now I realized that my role, too, was being "measured." The chair said that I was no longer just a student but was also not ready to be ascribed the role of "teacher."

I composed a silly poem to celebrate this realization.

Ban'ge zhuanjia (Half an Expert)

Foreign Affairs ponders on my role—
half a teacher and half a scholar,
half an expert: *ban'ge zhuanjia*
"In a dormitory room
the expert has a sofa chair.
We've looked here, and we've looked there,
but can't find half a chair anywhere!
Oh lookie here! In grubby apricot brocade
with broken arm, a little worn for wear,
half an expert chair."
I'm *ban'ge zhuanjia.*
It's witty and it suits me well, for
my Chinese friends think all is fair

when they see me in that wonky chair.
Confucius would be proud.
He'd see the chair and say aloud,
"Foreign Affairs' choice is proper and true,
This lady has got exactly her due."

THANK YOU VERY MUCH

Dru C. Gladney

1984

Late at night, or sometimes very early in the morning—in any case, nearly every time I passed through the entrance of the Ningxia Teacher's College in Yinchuan, Ningxia, where I was housed while doing my research in anthropology—Mr. Zhang, the gatekeeper, would greet me with the phrase *san kuai rou gei ni mu chi*, which sounded to me like "three pieces of meat for your mother to eat." I answered—or felt like answering—"Thank you Mr. Zhang, but my mother is in the U.S. and has plenty to eat." The strange exchange kept recurring, from early September until late October 1984. Then, on a train ride to Lanzhou, in Gansu, the train conductor helped me to figure out what Mr. Zhang had always been saying. It was also a clue to the puzzle of how Muslims in China (and perhaps elsewhere) manage to recite long passages of the Qur'an without knowing Arabic.

On the twelve-hour ride from Yinchuan to Lanzhou, as I chatted with my fellow passengers, word somehow reached the conductor that a foreigner with limited Chinese was on the train. About six hours into the trip, he summoned me to meet with him at the front of our railcar. I had only recently been permitted to live and travel in China's northwest, much of which was still "not open" to foreigners, so was a bit nervous about meeting with the conductor. I tried politely to decline the invitation, but to no avail. The conductor used offers of tea and snacks to lure me to sit with him, then pulled out a well-worn booklet that contained snippets of English, *hanyu pinyin*, and Chinese characters scrawled throughout. He asked me to teach him English phrases like: "Your tickets, please," "Please sit down," "The bathroom is at the end of the car," and "Next stop is Lanzhou." He not only asked for the phrases but wanted me to carefully repeat each word, syllable by syllable. For each, he wrote down a Chinese character that approximated the sound that he heard. When it was hard to match sound with a character, we tried to use *hanyu pinyin*, and that's when I learned that his *pinyin* wasn't very good. He reverted to Chinese characters, drawing on a long list to try to find the best match.

When we reached Lanzhou, I went to visit the central mosque in the city. I remembered being impressed on my first visit there in October 1983 by how the young students (known as *man la* "mullah"—in Arabic, "teacher") had managed to memorize long passages from the Qur'an. Like all Muslims in China's Hui community, they had grown up speaking local Chinese dialects and had been required to learn the language of their holy book much as I had memorized Latin phrases while serving as a Catholic altar boy. They had proudly shown me a twelve-year-old acolyte who had memorized the entire Quran that way. Having learned something from my ride on the train, I asked on this occasion to see their Arabic primers, and sure enough, under each word were scrawled small Chinese characters that approximated the sounds of the Arabic. The head of the mosque, Imam Ma Shixiong, later explained to me that only after students had managed to memorize long passages from the Qur'an by rote would he begin to teach them the meanings of the sacred texts.

When I returned to the front gate of the Teacher's College in Yinchuan, and Mr. Zhang again warmly greeted me, instead of declining his kind offer to provide meat for my mother, this time I told him, "You are welcome Mr. Zhang!" Then we spent a few hours working together to write down the Chinese characters that best recorded the sounds of that phrase: *yu ah wei li kun!*

悟

WHERE ARE WE GOING?

Thomas D. Gorman

1984

In 1984, I visited Sichuan province at the invitation of the provincial foreign trade bureau to write a report for a European magazine on Sichuan's trade, investment, and tourism potential. Weeks in advance, I had asked my contact person in Chengdu to find me a map of the province to assist with my writing and illustrating the article.

On arrival, I learned that he had not yet found me a map. We visited the largest local Xinhua Bookstore together, but they said they did not sell maps. The staff seemed surprised and somewhat shocked that someone—especially a foreigner—would inquire about buying a map. I had no alternative but to begin the series of local travels to different cities and towns in various parts of the province without a map.

I was given a multiday itinerary that listed our various destinations, but there were no details on where they were—not even "about four hours north by car," "six hours southwest by rail," or the like. I wanted some geographical perspective, so before we left Chengdu for the first destination, I asked our liaison man about each of the main towns we would visit: roughly how far it was in travel time, and in what general direction. I made a note of his answers. Later, I asked another member of our entourage the same question, but his answers were very different, so I asked several others after that. I found to my surprise that there was a huge variance among their answers. These were people from the bureau or its affiliated organizations who were generally very friendly and helpful, treating me for the most part like a guest. I could fathom no plausible reason for them to be dishonest about directions.

As we traveled—by car, van, and train—I came to realize that my first visits to these places in their home province were their own first visits as well. Ordinary Chinese people at the time had near zero mobility in their living and working routines. If they went somewhere, it was ordered and organized by some higher authority, and that didn't seem to happen much. They thus had no need for or interest in maps. Apart from ordinary people's lack of interest, maps had been deemed state secrets, along with the weather report, ostensibly because of their potential value to foreign military enemies.

I realized that, growing up in the United States, a highly mobile society, I had taken access to maps for granted. You could buy a map of your home state in just about any gas station, and local TV news regularly depicted scenes—identified by place—from around the city or region in which you lived. Learning to drive a car provided an incentive to acquire knowledge of how to read a road map. The explosion in popularity of hiking, camping, and other outdoor sports beginning in the 1960s created wider demand for topographical, state, and national park maps.

In the early 1980s, huge swaths of China were still off-limits to tourism. This would of course gradually change, as would the availability of locally published maps for sale at the retail level. One of the striking changes over the ensuing decades has been the increased mobility of ordinary Chinese people, and with it, geographic knowledge of their surroundings.

悟

OLD LADY

Stanley Rosen

1985

My first trip to Xi'an was in 1980, and I visited there regularly beginning in 1985 as I served, about a dozen times, as a scholar-escort for delegations sent by the National Committee on US-China Relations. On my 1985 trip, I was wandering around near my hotel, the People's Hotel, a massive Stalinist architectural structure opened in 1953 and one of the few places then available for foreigners to stay in Xi'an. (In 2014 it was transformed into the five-star Sofitel Legend People's Grand Hotel.)

As I was walking around to get a better feel of all the activities within the city wall, including the exciting Muslim quarter, I found myself in front of a small state store selling local handicrafts, imitation terra-cotta warriors, and paintings and calligraphy. I was about to enter when I noticed a short middle-aged woman sitting in front of the store, also selling paintings, paper cuts, and calligraphy. It was still the relatively early days of the *getihu*—meaning people who had no work unit (*danwei*) and were simply trying to make a living selling anything for which there might be a market, including clothing, watermelons, or daily-use goods. Such people had very low social status, and a fair number had been in prison or had otherwise problematic backgrounds.

I began talking with the woman about her life and inspecting her merchandise, which she was selling for three *yuan* per item—a price obviously far lower than those of the relatively similar goods in the state store. She told me that she had done the paper cuts, her husband was a calligrapher, and her son had done the paintings. As I was about to make a purchase, she suddenly jumped up and moved to the center of the sidewalk. Instinctively, I followed her, and we were immediately surrounded by a group of nasty-looking, burly men who were far from friendly.

It was clear that at a minimum they wanted to confiscate her goods. Instead, she handed them to me, leaving the men—who I assumed to be an early plainclothes version of the dreaded *chengguan*, established in 2001 to keep order in the urban areas and still feared by urban peddlers—to assess the implications of confronting a foreigner. Having seen the stalls of food vendors in Xi'an overturned, presumably because they were operating without a license, I quickly assessed this to be a similar situation. After a tense standoff of five or ten minutes when no one moved or said anything, they eventually left.

The "power" of a foreigner to stand up to official China was a revelation to this woman, and she treated me as her benefactor. From that time on, every year when I went to Xi'an with a National Committee group, I would arrange for her, often with her son, to come to my hotel room where they would display their wares for delegation members, who loved the give-and-take of Chinese-style bargaining. In those days, there were two kinds of Chinese *renminbi*—the regular kind and the kind called "foreign exchange certificates" that were needed to purchase imported goods. And which did the little lady prefer? Neither. She liked U.S. dollars. I think as much as anything, it was the liveliness of this tiny pepper pot, who was so garrulous (with a very heavy local accent) and visibly delighted when she received

U.S. dollars and immediately hid them in her clothing, that resonated with the delegation members. Indeed, one former Fulbright delegation member gave me twenty dollars to give to her the next time I was in Xi'an, which of course I did, although I had a difficult time making her understand why someone she didn't even remember would want to give her twenty dollars.

Over the years, I visited their one-room apartment, with very little ventilation, on numerous occasions and saw the family gradually improve their situation as China's reforms began to take off in the 1990s and selling paintings and paper cuts to foreigners became more acceptable. Her son, for example, began to show up on his motorcycle.

I missed one year, 2005, when I didn't make it to Xi'an, but I called the next summer and was told that she had passed away the year before. As her son related her death, he said that, although ill, she anxiously waited all that summer of 2005, certain of my arrival with a new delegation at any time, but it was not to be, and she was gone by the autumn.

Part V

悟

Reading Tea Leaves

By the middle of the 1980s, more and more foreign visitors were gaining greater access to China. While economic growth raised standards of living, economic deregulation and the dismantling of many state-owned enterprises also brought instability and uncertainty. Some in China debated the dangers of Western ideas amid a flood of cultural imports. While Deng Xiaoping clearly remained the paramount leader of China, he did not hold the Party chairmanship or the presidency, and the formal reins of power were held by the energetic reformers, Hu Yaobang and Zhao Ziyang. As the economy roared, many wondered how long "opening and reform" could last before a reckoning between the vibrant new energy of the post-Mao decade and some of the more reactionary and anxious Party elders emerged. The trend toward ever more space for intellectual expression peaked in 1985, when, for example, the Chinese Writers Association was allowed for the first and only time to elect its own leaders. The tide turned, though, when a crackdown on student demonstrations in 1986 and the brutal massacre of demonstrators in Beijing on June 4, 1989, ended the intellectual openness in dramatic fashion. Beginning then, the government's message to the Chinese people was essentially, "Make money and be patriotic, but keep quiet in public about politics, religion, or unapproved thoughts."

悟

BOOKS ON SECONDARY EXTRACTION

Geoffrey Ziebart

1985

I was working with a Canadian petroleum-consulting firm that the Canadian International Development Agency (CIDA) had engaged to help extract oil reserves in the famous Daqing oilfield, which was China's largest. In northeastern China, Daqing had been so successful that, during the Cultural Revolution, Mao Zedong had urged all of Chinese industry to "Learn from Daqing." In the mid-1980s, the area still had plenty of oil underground, but the easy extraction had all been done, and what remained could be had only by much more difficult "secondary extraction." The Canadian consulting firm was one of the best in the world at secondary extraction, and CIDA's role was to help China by bringing the consultants and the Daqing oil people together.

In 1985, Daqing sent a delegation of petroleum engineers, geologists, political leaders, and others to Calgary. They clearly were excited to be meeting with world-class experts. The Canadian side decided to purchase a number of the leading books on geology, drilling, and secondary extraction as a present to the Chinese delegation. The books were very expensive, but the Canadians knew how valuable they could be to their visitors. The Chinese delegation leader expressed his thanks. This all made sense to me.

Shortly thereafter, though, some of the junior experts on the Chinese side asked me if I could get copies for them, too. I was bewildered. The books were expensive; why would they need duplicates? So I asked, and the junior people explained that the original set would sit on the bookshelf in the delegation leader's office and that he would not allow them access. He was the Communist Party representative, and therefore the senior official on the delegation, but he knew little about oil extraction and would not be reading the books. Still, he was the leader, and in the world he inhabited, it would be important that the books be visible on the bookshelves in his office. It followed that he would not (could not?) let others remove them.

Nowadays everything is online, so a particular book is not as important as before. But in that day, in 1985, China was much poorer than it is now, and such books were the dreams of engineers. I asked the senior Canadian liaison if we could buy another set of books for the people who would do the actual work. He said there was no more in the budget; besides, "Why can't they borrow from the Party leader's office?" As I sighed at the futility of trying to explain the Chinese dynamics to him, I pictured in my mind's eye those young Chinese engineers looking wistfully from the corridor at those wonderful, expensive books—paid for by my Canadian tax dollars—that were going to waste because the person who possessed them believed that to allow others to remove them would diminish his power and prestige.

MAKING ASSUMPTIONS

Jeffrey N. Wasserstrom

1986–1987

When I bring up my first trip to China in essays, books, or lectures, I often focus on a few days in December 1986, when I witnessed part of a student protest wave that began in Hefei and crested in Shanghai, where I was midway through an academic year devoted to PhD dissertation research on Chinese history. When I think back to that trip, though, three specific moments in earlier months—August, October, and January—pop into my mind. They have little to do with one another except that, in each case, a faulty assumption relating to identity (in one case a cab driver's assumption about mine, in the other cases mine about Chinese people with whom I was interacting) was revealed. I present them here as three vignettes.

VIGNETTE ONE

August 1986. My wife and I arrive in Shanghai, never having set foot in any part of China before, and the initial experience is unimaginably disorienting. We know we need to get some local currency, but we can't figure out how to do that, and my classroom-learned Mandarin isn't much help. Although a period of "reform and opening" was proclaimed almost a decade earlier, and the guidebooks we read before coming insist that Shanghai is still, as it had long been, China's "most cosmopolitan city," there are very few other foreigners around and no guidance in the form of signs to help those of us who are there. The Hongqiao airport offers no indication of where to exchange dollars for *yuan*, and no one seems to understand what I am getting at when I refer to *yuan* by its formal label *renminbi*. I think it might be an issue of accent or tones (never my strong point) or maybe dialect (I know that Shanghainese is distinctive), but I later find out it is mostly just that everyone refers to *kuai* (*kuai* is to *yuan* roughly what bucks are to dollars).

The next challenge is to find a taxi in the pothole-filled parking lot outside the terminal, and then to get a driver to agree to take us to Fudan University. The second part is not easy, but not because of a language problem. The first three drivers recognize the name of the place when I say it, but it is in an out-of-the-way semi-rural district (the metropolis has by now sprawled out to incorporate the area, but it hadn't then), and they do not want to go there because of a fear that no one will hire them to drive back into the city. Thankfully, the fourth driver nods okay, a bit grudgingly, but he seems a good-natured fellow.

As soon as we are in the cab, he proves just how eager to please us he is by trying to do something nice. But it backfires. He puts a tape in his cassette deck, looks back at us, and smiles. He seems sure he is doing something that we will find a real treat. Suddenly, music is blaring out of the speakers. A male singer with strong vocal cords is belting out words that neither of us can understand. It isn't English, Chinese, or French—my wife, Anne, knows French. It's Italian.

The driver, by looking at us, has concluded that we are a young couple from the West (so far so good) and hence probably not fans of the Chinese opera featured on most of his cassette tapes (correct again). Where he goes astray is to assume that we must be fans of Luciano Pavarotti, who has recently gained a considerable following among urban Chinese, including many in their midtwenties, just like us. A collection of the singer's arias is the only tape of "Western music" he owns, so he has put it on and cranked up the volume (perhaps because he has read that young Westerners like to listen to their music loud). We recognize his gesture as a well-meaning and hospitable one, but a Chinese phrase one of my graduate school professors is fond of comes to mind: it definitely doesn't "scratch where it itches." Hearing Joni Mitchell, Diana Ross, Willie Nelson, or Elvis Costello while look- ing out at the many unfamiliar sights outside the window—such as people working to repair a stretch of road under spotlights of the sort that, growing up in L.A., I associated with films being shot, or bamboo scaffolding on the outside of buildings under construction—would have been comforting. Hearing Pavarotti was not.

VIGNETTE TWO

October 1986. I have made a friend, Xinyong, who is doing graduate work in world history. We discover that we have many common inter- ests despite having grown up in very different worlds and, although the same age, in some senses in different times. He had rarely ridden in a car, and I had never labored on a farm the way he did when sent to the countryside late in the Cultural Revolution. I met Anne when we were students at the same college, while he met his wife, Fei, when they were sent to work in the same village. We often start conversa- tions expecting to have to work to arrive at shared frames of reference, or even understanding of terms, which is fine, sometimes even fun.

Sometimes, though, one of us gets befuddled. This happens when we feel as though we are speaking the same language—which for us is a back-and-forth mix of Chinese and English, as we have roughly comparable skills in the other's native tongue—and then one of us realizes something strange is actually going on. This happens dur- ing a conversation that begins with me saying that I feel that being a Californian (I was born in Palo Alto, grew up in Santa Monica, was an undergrad at UC Santa Cruz, and am midway through the Berkeley doctoral program) sets me apart from other Americans in some ways. He nods. He feels the same way about his ties to Shandong. I say Californians are more likely to be X, Y, and Z than people from some other states. He gives related Shandong examples. (I can't remember the details either of us offered.) Then I bring up food: when I moved to Boston to do a master's, I say, I found that Californians were more used to eating avocados and artichokes. He nods again. He says that there is something special about Shandong *jiaozi* (dumplings). They are the best. And since he is from Shandong, next time I come over, he'll prove it. I love *jiaozi*, so say that sounds like an excellent plan.

Then the strange thing happens. "By the way," I ask, "when were you last in Shandong?" "Oh, I've never been there," he says, "but my father grew up there." You can't be a Californian American without having set foot in California, but you could refer to yourself as an Irish American without having been to Ireland, so I consider that being Shandong-Chinese might be more comparable to the latter than the former, something that had never occurred to me.

VIGNETTE THREE

January 1987. We need to get Anne's visa renewed so we go to a government building where we are helped by a young man who is friendly, wears a police uniform, and speaks impeccable English. (If only, I think, he had been the first person I tried to talk to at the airport five months earlier! Thank goodness Xinyong's English isn't this good, I also think, or I would never speak Chinese with him, and my language skills would improve even more slowly.) We talk about various things, and then I can't resist asking what may be a dicey question about politics, in part because this is the first time we have been downtown since watching big protest marches there a few weeks before. I'm wondering if he was on duty when police turned out to warn students that the government's willingness to let youths let off some steam by demonstrating was ending and that there would be arrests if things went on.

"Were you out there," I ask, pointing to the place where students had demonstrated, "when the protests were taking place?" He pauses for a minute, pondering my question, and I worry that I've asked something I shouldn't have. "Only in my heart," he eventually replies, a wistful look in his eyes. His answer makes it clear that, in his mind, it was the fact that he was the same age as the protesters and had similar hopes and grievances, not that they were students and he was a policeman, that mattered and presumably inspired my question.

I'm not sure the taxi driver came away from our ride with him feeling that he needed to rethink his assumptions about the musical tastes of "Westerners," but I do know that hearing Xinyong's comment about Shandong is one thing I think about when I begin classes on Chinese history by saying that in some ways it is better to think of China as comparable to the continent of Europe than as comparable to a single country in it. I may sometimes forget the lesson I learned from the policeman's comment, but I try not to. When interacting with Chinese people since then, I strive to keep in mind, as it is worth keeping in mind in other settings, too, of course, that focusing too much on the clothes someone is wearing may lead you to make the wrong assumption about the things they care about.

悟

INTERNAL DOCUMENT

Stanley Rosen

1986

In 1986, I spent six months doing interviews and library research on issues related to Chinese youth, social change, and education in Beijing, Hangzhou, and Guangzhou. My host in Guangzhou was the South China Normal Institute (now a university). One interviewee was a sixteen-year-old student at the high school attached to the university. It was widely considered to be the best high school in Guangzhou. The student was the head of the school's student union.

One evening I asked him if he could get me a copy of the preference form that students filled out when they listed their preferences in universities and departments as part of the process of applying for university. He told me that he should be able to do so and that I should meet him in two days at the English corner in a café next to the Guangzhou Public Library.

I showed up at the appointed time and found a table in the café, which was extremely crowded, because the English corner in those days was very popular with high school and university students. The student soon arrived with what looked like something thicker than a university preference form. He placed it in front of me, face up, and the first thing I noticed were the characters for *mimi* (secret) at the top of the mimeographed document. Since foreigners always attracted a crowd at English corners, and I had already told several aspirant language learners that I was waiting for someone, I quickly glanced around to see if anyone had noticed the arrival of this document. It crossed my mind, just barely, that I might somehow have done something wrong during my months in China and now was being set up. I was relieved to see that apparently no one was observing this exchange.

I then turned the document over to the back, which was blank. Still unaware of what this document actually was, I asked the student whether it was okay for a foreigner to see it. I kept my voice low. He said that he had asked the Communist Youth League (CYL) assistant who had given him the document—a young woman about his age, who was also studying at the high school—whether it was okay for a foreigner to have the material. She asked him whether it was a foreign friend or a foreign spy, and he responded that it was a foreign friend. She said that in that case, it was okay to give it to him.

When I got back to my room and examined the document, it turned out to be a list of many work units in Guangzhou, with statistics on the number of CYL members, the percentage of youth league members in the unit who had become Communist Party members, and similar types of statistical information on the CYL. It wasn't what I asked for, but I wasn't complaining. I was only wondering whether I should try and take the document out of China.

I decided to do so, and after six months of traveling around China and collecting books, bound journals, photocopies, and other heavy material, I had four large suitcases, which meant that when I left Guangzhou for Hong Kong I could only go by overnight ferry, which I did, joining a very long line of Cantonese—I saw no other foreigners boarding the ferry—and despite some efforts by customs officers to reach into the suitcases, I arrived safely back in Hong Kong after my very successful research trip.

BROTHERHOOD

Geoffrey Ziebart

1987

When I was a student at Fudan University in Shanghai in the mid-1980s, I had already studied some Japanese Aikido and wanted to look into the Chinese martial arts. The Shanghai Institute of Physical Culture was nearby, so I went to introduce myself and asked if I could train. The students at the institute were effusive in their welcome. They were working toward what amounted to bachelor's degrees in San Da, a martial art that combines kicking, punching, grappling, and throwing. They had bodies like Bruce Lee's and were skilled contact fighters, not just guys making cool moves in *wushu*—the generic name for China's martial arts.

Boy, were they were tough. As an example, a teammate sat down after winning a bout in a tournament one day, with what appeared to be an extra joint between his elbow and wrist. "Shit," he said, "I just broke my arm." Apparently he hadn't noticed until he sat down. Although they were at a school and were earning degrees, they were hardly academics. One of them, my best friend in the group, complained that they had to write a graduate thesis of *three thousand characters*! That's maybe 2,300 words in English—hardly a tome, especially for a graduation thesis. Part of their problem may have been that years of punching had left their knuckles so swollen that they had difficulty holding pens.

After our training sessions, a few of us often retreated to a local hotel restaurant for dinner. I felt honored and privileged that these tough guys would welcome a tall, skinny foreigner—who played volleyball but was a novice at martial arts—into their group.

Fast-forward five years. On a business trip in 1992, I met up again with that best friend of mine. He had since become a police officer in a city in Zhejiang province, where his duties included traveling to other provinces to secure the rendition of wanted suspects. Warm as ever in his welcome to me, he invited me to Hangzhou for his wedding. He also told a story and made a request.

The story was that five years earlier, when our San Da group had graduated and was enjoying a final, celebratory night together at our accustomed hotel restaurant, a neighboring table of regulars apparently had insulted me as a foreigner. I was utterly unaware of the insult, but my buddies took note. A few days later, after I had left China, they went again to that hotel restaurant, found the offenders, and delivered them a proper thrashing.

The story surprised me: What? I hadn't even noticed the insult. And if I had, would it warrant an actual beating? My friend beamed as he answered, "No way! They insulted you, so we went back for them,

and we found them . . . and bodies went flying and tables flipping!"
He described the scene in detail.

Didn't the ruckus bring the police? Perhaps it did, he answered, but
he and his buddies had foreseen that danger. They had waited until
their last night in Shanghai to take action. They cleaned out their dorm
rooms, packed, and went to the restaurant. After the thrashing, they
paid their bill, picked up their bags, went to the train station, and left
for Anhui, Zhejiang, and elsewhere.

Why did they do this? I had already left China, unaware of any insult. What was the point? The episode gave me new insight into what
"brother" means in this Chinese subculture. It shows the lengths to
which brothers will go for brothers, and that the connection is almost
metaphysical. They do something "for" you, yes, and you don't need
to thank them for doing it. You don't have to know about it. They are
just as happy if you never know about it. It may only be because my
friend, on the eve of his wedding, was a bit tipsy that he let me know
what my brothers had done for me—on principle.

That was the story he told. The request was this: he wanted me, the
next evening, at his wedding banquet, to be his "drinking substitute."
As groom he would have to go to every banquet table to do toasts.
If he drank at every one, he explained, he would end up hopelessly
inebriate—which would not look good and also would detract from
his performance with his wife on their wedding night, which could
hardly please her. So I agreed. We went to thirteen tables, where I
drank for him. It was *maotai* hard liquor. I don't know how I survived.
But it was an unquestionable duty. I was his brother. Fighting? Drinking? Even dying? What did it matter? A brother.

MICKEY MOUSE AT PEKING U

David Moser

1988

It was 1988, and I found myself at Peking University taking part in a
book translation project, my collaborators being a handful of Peking

University's brightest graduate students. Deng Xiaoping's opening up was about a decade on, and it was interesting for me to observe which of the myriad foreign books and ideas these Chinese intellectuals gravitated to. The bookstores and outdoor bookstalls were piled with translations of everyone from Gabriel Garcia Marquez to Dale Carnegie, from the Holy Bible to L. Ron Hubbard's *Scientology*. It seemed that Chinese publishing was making up for three lost decades by flooding the market with anything and everything the West had to offer.

Books were one thing, but foreign media such as movies and television were another. Compact discs and DVDs had not come to China, and the Internet was only a distant rumor. Commercial Chinese television was still in its infancy, and the initial influx of foreign TV offerings was random, chaotic, and sometimes bizarre. One early American TV show broadcast on Chinese TV was the idiotic sitcom *My Favorite Martian* (*Huoxing shushu Mading*), and I still remember vividly that the clumsily dubbed episodes were for some reason missing the laugh track, which gave them an interesting theater-of-the-absurd quality.

My Chinese friends had access to only one battered black-and-white TV set, in an activity room of a student dorm. Though students would crowd around the television set during soccer telecasts, for the most part they were fairly indifferent to the tame offerings of CCTV. Therefore, my curiosity was piqued one week when I suddenly noticed some of my student friends rushing out of the cafeteria, rice bowls in hand, in a hurry to get to the dorm TV room before 6:00.

"What's the rush?" I asked one of them. "What comes on at 6:00?"

"Mickey Mouse," he said.

Indeed, some of the classic Disney cartoons from the 1950s and 1960s, dubbed in Mandarin, had begun to appear on Beijing TV. But I was a bit puzzled by my friends' enthusiasm for these cultural artifacts. I asked my friend Liu, who was reading Kafka and translating German philosophy in his spare time, "What's the appeal of Mickey Mouse cartoons?"

"For us, they are a window into another world," he said. "They show us that society can be ordered in a completely different way."

This seemed to me rather grandiose, to say the least, so the next day I joined him in front of the TV set at 6:00, waiting to see these cartoons from my childhood through the eyes of my Chinese academic friends. Viewed with a fresh perspective and listening to the comments and observations of the students, I began to see how Disney's vision indeed represented a kind of microcosm of a different cultural worldview.

In the Mickey Mouse world, all authority figures were pompous fools. The police were pictured as incompetent buffoons who could easily be hoodwinked and bullied. Classrooms were chaotic spaces where teachers were mocked and subjected to spitwad attacks. Mickey and Minnie Mouse could smooch and spoon openly in front of friends without embarrassment. Children were on equal footing with adults; Huey, Dewey, and Louie could sass their Uncle Donald Duck with impunity. Protagonists often found themselves in perilous situations, but somehow always escaped through creative leaps of imagination. And rules and conventions—even the very laws of physics—could be circumvented if one had enough self-confidence or sheer gumption.

"We've grown up absorbing movies and children's books that always contain a moral," Liu explained to me. "Everything we're fed encourages us to *ting hua*, to behave. These cartoons encourage us to see the world as open possibilities, not fixed realities."

悟

READING TEA LEAVES

Richard P. Madsen

1988–1989

From September 1988 to early January 1989, I was a visiting scholar at the Institute for American Studies at the Chinese Academy of Social Sciences in Beijing. The institute was on the thirteenth floor of the old Academy Building. Next to it was a much larger institute, the Institute of Marxism-Leninism-Mao Zedong Thought. I played on the American Institute's basketball team, and we were beaten badly by our much larger neighbor. The word went out that "America was defeated by Marxism-Leninism." I thought the saying contained a grain of truth— American liberalism up against ideological Chinese Marxism—but that was wrong. Many of the American-studies people were actually somewhat conservative, and many of the Marxism-Leninism-Mao Zedong Thought scholars were actually more radical dissenters. They were like theologians who had lost their faith. A few days before I left in early January, a scholar from the Marxism-Leninism Institute offered to take me to meet their director, Su Shaozhi. We rode on a pedicab through dangerous traffic to meet at Su's house. Su had just published a critique of the Chinese system in the *World Economic Herald* (a Shanghai journal that Jiang Zemin, the city's Party secretary, suppressed after prodemocracy demonstrations started in the spring of 1989). Su said that he now realized that all his writings about Marxism had been wrong. (After the June 4 massacre, he escaped into exile in America.)

Later, my Marxism-Leninism friend said he wanted to take me to a place where there weren't listening devices. We ended up at Perry Link's apartment at the Friendship Hotel (I don't know why he thought there were no listening devices there), where, while chain-smoking cigarettes, which annoyed Perry, he predicted some things that would happen in the coming year. The country was seething with discontent, he said, and sometime in the coming year, probably around one of the anniversaries of the 1919 May Fourth Movement or the 1949 founding of the PRC, there would be a major uprising. The government would probably put it down with force and declare martial law, and there would be serious repression for a long time to come. It was as if he was giving me a parting gift—the truth. I wrote this all down in my notebook. When I left China, I gave a talk at the Universities Service Center in Hong Kong and told them what I had heard. I also talked about it at the Harvard East Asian Research Center, where I was a visiting scholar for the spring semester. But no one took it seriously. I was too inexperienced in Chinese affairs and unduly alarmist. The experts knew that the system was stable.

EATING BITTERNESS

Vera Schwarcz

1989

Our children were playing together wordlessly on the marble barge in the middle of No Name Lake at Peking University in the spring of 1989. My old classmate from the Chinese Department, during my research year in 1979–1980, now had a seven-year-old girl, and I had come back to the university, with my five-year-old son, to attend a series of conferences about the 1919 May Fourth Movement. Unexpectedly, I was about to learn more about Chinese life than in all the academic conversations that were swirling about me at that time.

My classmate had been in the last group of worker-peasant students to be sent, in 1976, to China's premier university because of her "good" political background. She came from a poor family of uneducated manual laborers. We had become close friends while sitting together in literature classes. (I had chosen to be affiliated with the Chinese Department because the History Department was mired in dogmatic debates about class struggle.)

I treasured my friend for her open smile, nonjudgmental conversation, and readiness to help in any way that she could to make my life in our rough dormitory a bit easier. This meant bringing me hot water from the communal spigot two buildings away when I was sick and some fruits on the rare days when these were available in the student cafeteria. She was a short, strong young woman of twenty-two, and we had worked together well during the obligatory day of "labor"— harvesting wheat. This was the last year during which Peking University students had been required to muddy their shoes in the fields of a nearby commune.

Now, a decade later, we were both mothers. She had married a couple of years after graduating from university. It was considered a move "up" since she had found a skilled laborer making good money who was willing to build a life with a brainy girl. Within a year of their wedding, she gave birth to a baby girl, not a son. That started the daily beatings. They came during the harshest years of the one-child policy. The consequences of the policy were playing out in a brutal fashion in my friend's home, day after day.

The beatings were continuing every day as we spoke near the marble barge at the university. And she had not collapsed. As I looked into her tear-filled eyes and smiling face, I learned something about *chiku* (eating bitterness), something I had not actually witnessed during twenty-five years of teaching and writing about Chinese history.

I had often thought of *chiku* as a performance act—something orchestrated by the Communist Party in its political campaigns. There, peasants were coached to recite the terrible evils suffered at the hands of landlords before the "liberation" of 1949. In the spring of 1989, I had not yet read about the "incorrect" confusions that had happened in the late 1950s—when peasants sometimes spoke of their current hungers and terrors, forgetting to mention the bad old days.

All I understood as my friend shared her pain was that she was not consumed by her own daily eating of bitterness. Yes, her body was suffering pain; yes, her husband's violent reactions to her failure to bear a son had marked and marred her arms, legs, and back. Yet she was grateful to be a mother. She cherished that little girl in pigtails who was playing with my son. In this child lay hope for a different future.

Scholars have often argued that *chiku* is a special quality that somehow accounts for the longevity of Chinese culture itself. Here I saw that it could shorten a life just as readily as it might extend that of the larger society. More striking still was neither longevity nor endurance. It was literally a gut-level challenge to Western notions of how one deals with trauma and grief. We often assume that suffering leads to emotional indigestion—that it disturbs the "natural" ecology of the inner self. Yet here was my friend: in tears and triumphant at the same time.

After the tanks came into Tiananmen Square a couple of weeks after our children's play date, we did not meet again. Yet my old classmate had left me a template for looking at my own grief about the murder of unarmed students and the harsh crackdown at Peking University that followed. I, too, was learning how to *chiku*—to cry and to cherish the possibility of hope for another generation of youth, all at the same time.

Even if still unrealized, that hope has not soured in my mind, my mouth, or my stomach. If I can write these words, it is because a short, stocky, strong woman with no intellectual pretensions had taught me more than my decades of work on the tragic history of science and democracy in China.

悟

FROM CLAYDERMAN TO CUI JIAN

James A. Cook

1991

In the fall of 1991, as a graduate student in Chinese studies, I was heading to China for the first time. I had worked hard on Chinese language and felt at least semi-prepared on that score, but I didn't know how else to get ready. The videos that today are easy to find on YouTube and Youku weren't there then. There were pamphlets on how to get through a train station or apply for a residence card, but little that would help a person understand how different Chinese daily life would be.

And then there was my music. I loved it. From my years in San Francisco, I especially loved alternative music: from 1960s psychedelia to punk rock concerts with the Dead Kennedys at the Fab Mab, we Bay Area people were proud of ourselves as musical explorers. But looking at China? What should I expect? I found some Chinese recordings at a music shop in Tijuana, but they turned out to be Cultural Revolution paeans to Chairman Mao. What was music like in post-Mao China? I didn't know.

I decided that, to be safe, I had better bring along some music of my own. I packed sixty CDs and a boom box. I thought my classmates in the University of California's Education Abroad Program would be like-minded, but when we gathered at the San Francisco airport, I found that this was not at all the case. They were lasered in on advancing their Chinese as much as possible. Better to listen to Chinese music on the radio, they thought. The way they looked down on me and my boom box made me nervous. Had I made a spectacular mistake?

At Peking University, we settled into our dormitories at the foreign-student ghetto known as the Shao Yuan, or "Spoon Garden." I was shocked to find that my Chinese was not as strong as I had hoped. I was assigned to the "elementary level," where drills in speaking, reading, and listening filled my days. I sweated it out. No matter how bad my "China day," my recourse and salve in the evening was my music.

I was curious about China's music scene. Was it Chinese folk songs? Opera? How could I have guessed that it would be a Richard Clayderman frenzy? I had always thought of Clayderman's music, which the artist himself called "easy-listening arrangements of popular classical music," as something that my grandmother enjoyed. Romance and strings. In the mid-1980s, Clayderman's heavily advertised *Music of Love* album included arrangements of *Romeo and Juliet* and *Evita* and could be had in New York's Grand Central Station for $9.98 on 8-track, record, or cassette. But now, in the early 1990s, he might have been the most well-known contemporary Western musician in Asia. In Beijing, his music was seemingly everywhere—from the train station to university campuses to the big department stores on Wangfujing. According to a report in the *Shanghai Daily News*, Clayderman's "first Chinese concert in Beijing in 1992 was such a hit that his sheet music and recordings became best-sellers almost overnight. Euphoria about his piano playing could be heard everywhere in the country."

The Clayderman finding surprised not only me but also my classmates who had come to Beijing confident that "Chinese music on the radio" was the way to go. Two of them, Josh and Ken, retreated from their original position. One evening they knocked on my door offering a promise of food and beer in return for use of my boom box and CDs. Later, I heard sounds from the Minutemen's *Double Nickels on the Dime* floating from their room. I felt vindicated, of course, but still puzzled by the phenomenon of Clayderman in China.

By wonderful chance, I found some help one night at the disco at the Lido Holiday Inn, which was one of the few Beijing hotels in 1991–1992 that boasted a disco. With Josh, Ken, and a few other friends, I bumped into Cui Jian, who, as far as I was aware, was just another young musician. In fact, Cui was already known as the "father of Chinese rock 'n' roll." His first album, *Rock 'n' Roll on the New Long March*, was an enormous hit in early 1989, but he was not allowed to give concerts after he began supporting the prodemocracy demonstrations in Tiananmen Square that year. The Lido was one of the few places he could play music from his new album, *Solution.* We were astounded as we listened. Here was Chinese music that seemed indeed to be a "solution" to my Clayderman puzzle. Cui's songs used both traditional Chinese instruments and Western guitar to bring forth bold and exciting music. I saw, and still do see, his song "Let Me Go Berserk in the Snow" as the epitome of Chinese rock 'n' roll.

I realized, too, that my classmates had not been entirely wrong, back at the San Francisco airport, to suspect me of having feelings of cultural superiority. After that evening at the Lido, I saw China as reengaging with transnational popular culture, and I saw Richard Clayderman and Cui Jian both playing important roles. At a time when China's door to outside influences was still tightly controlled, and before the rise of the Internet, Clayderman and Cui were both taking crucial first steps. My sixty CDs represented my belief that China's music would not meet my modern tastes. But now I knew I had to venture beyond the Spoon Garden ghetto if I wanted to find modern Chinese music and find, too, that rock 'n' roll could be different in a different culture.

悟

CATHOLIC CHURCH IN TIANJIN

Richard P. Madsen

1992

In August 1992, I went to Tianjin to prepare to study the Catholic Church in China. My project was part of a package of five different projects of UC San Diego and the Tianjin Academy of Social Sciences, funded by the Luce Foundation. I knew my project was potentially the most "sensitive" of the projects, but I didn't realize *how* sensitive. When I got there, Li Shiyu, a distinguished elderly scholar of Chinese popular religion, welcomed me warmly and told me, "Tomorrow we'll go to the cathedral and talk to some of the priests." But when the official in charge of the project heard this, he said, "What!? We have to make some arrangements first." Then after a few days, he told me, "The local government says you can't go to any churches and can't talk to any Catholics." End of project. My return flight was a week and a half later, so I spent the next few days sightseeing. But I knew that the following Saturday, August 15, was the Feast of the Assumption of Mary—one of the biggest feast days for Chinese Catholics. I asked the director if I could just go to the church on that day and take some pictures. He reluctantly said yes, but "Just take some pictures, don't talk with anyone there."

They drove me with a bunch of handlers, and when we arrived at 7:00 a.m., the cathedral was packed with more than a thousand people. We barely managed to get seats in the last pew. The music was magnificent, the people extremely fervent, and the ceremony beautiful. It was a day when a hundred young children were receiving First Communion, the boys in red cassocks and girls in white dresses with little crowns of artificial flowers on their heads. (This was despite official regulations that children were not supposed to be given religious instruction.) I wondered, what would be so "sensitive" about this? After it was over, the handlers hurried me out, but I had time to notice a sign on the door warning that the church would be strictly closed on certain days. There was an ominous feel to it. I asked my handlers if I could at least take a few pictures of the children who had received First Communion. The Catholics coming out of the church were extremely helpful—"Stand over here to get the best view." Then we were gone. The next day was Sunday, and my handlers were off work. So I got a cab and went to the church myself. The church was again crowded and the Mass beautiful. After Mass, some Catholics approached me and said, "We saw you here yesterday taking pictures. Would you like to come back to the rectory and meet the bishop and see some more pictures?" So I went. They showed me videos of the previous day's event and photo albums of other activities of the church in the past year. They introduced me to the bishop and several priests, and they talked about the various activities depicted in the photo albums.

The next day at the Academy of Social Sciences, I didn't say anything about my time in the church and they didn't say anything to me. Later, they told me they would try to work something out so I could do some of my research project, and most importantly, they introduced me to Fan Lizhu, a young researcher who was interested in popular religion. She would later become a valuable helper and good friend. Then I returned home.

Back in the United States, I discovered some of the background to my visit in Tianjin. One of the most prominent and beloved of China's Catholic "underground bishops," Bishop Fan Xueyan, having been in and out of jail, was sentenced to a three-year prison term in 1989. The day before he was to have been released, he died. The prison said he had fallen and hurt his head. Catholics who saw the body said he had been beaten to death. There was a massive outcry among China's Catholics, especially in the Hebei area around Tianjin. The PLA had been called in to discourage people from going to his home village for his funeral, but ten thousand Catholics showed up anyway. This had happened just four months before I arrived. Meanwhile, the Tianjin diocese had appointed a new bishop, whom many underground Catholics considered illegitimate. The Tianjin Catholic community was extremely tense.

The following year, when I returned to do four months of fieldwork, some Catholics from the cathedral told me, "You know why we were so eager to help you that day when you were taking pictures of the first communion children? The underground Catholics were going to make a big disturbance that day, ruining the ceremony. But we told them, 'Look, there is a foreigner here taking pictures, it wouldn't be good to have a disturbance now.'"

I had wandered into a hornets' nest. The buzzing had died down somewhat by the time I returned in 1993, but the potential for an outburst was still there. We had worked out an arrangement where I wouldn't officially study Catholics, but we would study the "customs and habits" of villages that happened to be composed mostly of Catholics. We went to a place several hours away from Tianjin city, which consisted of two lineages, the Chens and the Lis. The Lis were all Catholic, and they had a handsome church, officially approved and affiliated with the Catholic Patriotic Association. The other half of the village belonged to the Chens. The Party secretary was a Chen, and he had started some cottage industries that mostly provided jobs for the Chens. After praising all the things he had done, we had a big lunch with him lubricated by lots of white liquor. At the end, we asked him if it would be all right to do some research in the village, and he agreed. We had a great time interviewing the Lis about their church. They also told us about the adjacent village, Hu village, which was also Catholic but mostly connected with the underground Church. We walked over and interviewed the local leader, who had built a little unapproved chapel in his house. That's when the hornets started buzzing again.

We were sitting with a leader of the Li Catholics—a simple adobe house with a dirt floor and lots of baby ducklings running around—when a black sedan drove up with two public security police. They played good cop and bad cop: "We are worried about your safety. You don't have permission to be here. Leave immediately." We responded, "Party Secretary Chen gave us permission" (although he had been drunk). They said, "You didn't ask the Public Security Bureau for permission." "We didn't know that was necessary." "It is." This was so unsettling that when I got up to leave, I accidently stepped on one of the ducklings and crushed it. The Catholic leader said, "Don't worry about it. And don't worry about the police. We know them. They come here all the time."

This necessitated a change in fieldwork strategy, but we had already learned a lot.

Part VI

悟

Welcome to
Our Foreign Friends

After the violent suppression of the 1989 Tiananmen Square protests, Chinese society was largely in the doldrums until, in 1992, Deng Xiaoping went to Shanghai, Guangzhou, and elsewhere on a "southern tour" aimed at rekindling interest in money making. The plan worked, and through the 1990s, China's economic boom revived and continued, although now the framework of strict one-party rule was firmly in place. The pace of growth was bewildering, although some harsh environmental and social consequences accompanied it. Meanwhile, the government was successful in encouraging nationalism as a twin public value along with money making. The nation cheered as the colonies of Hong Kong (1997, formerly under the United Kingdom) and then Macao (1999, formerly under Portugal) reverted to Chinese rule. Even while aspects of American popular culture were welcomed in China, many Chinese expressed frustration and resentment at policies in Washington that seemed to contain China and to obstruct Beijing's global influence. Amid these shifts of the geopolitical tectonic plates, foreigners visited China with increased latitude to travel without minders, and while warm welcomes were common, embarrassments and conflicts still occurred.

悟

WELCOME TO OUR FOREIGN FRIENDS

David Moser

1994

My first few years in China were spent mostly in academic settings, among enlightened students and teachers who were curious about the outside world and invariably friendly to foreigners. As an American making forays into the culture, I seldom experienced anything but general goodwill and the warmest of welcomes among the Chinese people I encountered. I remember thinking that no matter what conflicts our two governments might have, at least personal contacts between Chinese and American people are reliably friendly.

This *kumbaya* spell was broken for me in the fall of 1994 when I attended a conference on the Chinese oral performing art called Shandong *kuaishu* ("clappertales") at Linqing in Shandong province, where the art form was born. Two Japanese exchange students and I were accompanied by a Peking University professor who specialized in verbal folk arts. After a bumpy twelve-hour bus ride from Beijing, we arrived at Linqing around suppertime and checked into the hotel where the conference was being held. We three foreigners, like everyone else, followed the instructions of the conference organizers and went to the rooms to which they assigned us. We assumed the necessary formalities had been handled on a group basis.

But around 8:00 the next evening, as the two Japanese students and I were relaxing in our rooms, the Peking University professor burst in and said, "Get your passports and IDs and come downstairs with me. The police want to talk with us." I panicked for a moment when I realized that I had not brought my passport. I had attended other conferences with this professor, and no one had ever asked for my passport.

We were ushered into a room where some policemen were sitting on beds, smoking and watching a CCTV variety show. They rose to greet us and shook hands. Their breath smelled strongly of alcohol. They asked for our IDs. The Japanese students handed over their passports, and I handed over my student ID, which was all I could offer. A younger officer, who wore a black leather jacket, began to scrutinize the documents. An older officer wearing a thick green army overcoat began directing questions at one of the Japanese students.

"What time did you arrive in Linqing yesterday?" he asked.

"I don't remember the exact time," she said, her voice trembling.

"You arrived at 6:30 p.m.," the officer said. "And what time is it now?" We shrugged. None of us was wearing a watch. The officer pulled out a small clock and brandished it in front of us as if it were a piece of evidence at a murder trial.

"It is now 8:30 p.m.," he said. "Foreigners are required to register within 24 hours after arriving in a city that is outside their place of residence in China. Why didn't you register?"

"No one asked us to," the Japanese student said, defiantly but nervously. "We came as a group. We were just following everyone else. We assumed the conference people had taken care of the formalities."

The younger officer wearing the leather jacket spoke up. "Ignorance is no excuse," he said, pointing a finger at us. "You three are in violation of the laws of the People's Republic of China. You are now here in Linqing illegally. This is a serious violation." I glanced over at the Peking University professor and saw that his usually jocular face was white as a sheet.

The officer in the leather jacket addressed the Japanese students. "We may be a poor country compared to Japan, but that doesn't mean you can come here and ignore our laws, right?" The Japanese student who had been interrogated began to cry.

Then the officer in the green army coat turned to me. "The way I see it is, Mr. Mo here is in the most serious violation," he said. "Article xxx of the legal code of the People's Republic of China requires all foreigners when traveling to carry personal identification with them. You are now in violation of that code and are subject to prosecution." Then his voice took on a sarcastic edge. "You should understand this, Mr. Mo. You're from America, after all, and we all know that America is a country of laws, yes? You're in violation of our laws now."

My legs were trembling. I sensed that there was no use in trying to defend myself. I just mumbled, "Yes, I know. I'm sorry. It was just a mistake."

The policeman went on. "My suggestion is that we fine these two Japanese 500 *yuan* each for failing to register. The American here is a much more serious case. He is subject to a 5,000 *yuan* fine. Furthermore, since he is technically an unidentified foreigner, he's going to have to come down to the police station to spend the night there. He can't stay in this hotel." We all looked at each other in disbelief. Surely they weren't serious. The whole thing was just an oversight; we were hapless students attending an academic conference, not some drug smugglers caught red-handed in a deal!

The Peking University professor jumped into the fray and began to bargain with the police, at times animatedly sweet-talking them, at times defending our innocence and pleading for mercy. He volunteered to take full responsibility for the mixup, and, grabbing a piece of hotel stationery and a pen, volunteered to produce a written statement accepting full blame. The officers seemed somewhat willing to consider this solution, but haggled over the correct wording of the statement. The professor had to rewrite it several times.

They kept us there for two hours, intimidating us, making veiled threats, and scrutinizing our IDs over and over, as if they were ancient Buddhist texts. Several times throughout the course of their harangue, they would add, incongruously, "Of course we welcome our foreign friends, but our job is to protect you." (So why did we suddenly feel so unprotected when *they* showed up?)

Finally, through the window, we saw a jeep pull up outside the hotel and a higher-ranking officer got out. He strode into the room, took stock of the situation, and sent the inebriated cops on their way, scolding them with, "Quit causing a ruckus and get back to the station." He mumbled a terse apology to us, returned our IDs, and warned the professor, "These kids are your responsibility. If they get into any trouble, we can't help them."

For me and my fellow students, this was perhaps our first inkling of a widespread sense of nationalist resentment that would later surface in increasingly public form, with a spate of publications such as *China Can Say No* in 1996 and exploding into violence after the NATO bombing of the Chinese embassy in Belgrade in 1999.

悟

CRADLE OF THE REVOLUTION

Andrew D. Morris

1996

In 1996, while doing PhD dissertation research on the history of Republican-era sports and physical culture in China, I became enthralled at one point by some primary sources on sport in the early 1930s in the mountainous Communist base area on the Jiangxi-Hunan border. In order to see those materials, I needed to reach the collection's editor, a historian named Zeng Biao who worked at Gannan Normal University in Ganzhou, Jiangxi. I wrote him a letter asking if I could visit him and do an interview. He politely agreed and we set a date for December.

I decided to go to Ganzhou via Jinggangshan, the home of the famed Jiangxi Soviet founded in 1931. This "Cradle of the Revolution" held a fascinating place in the history of the Communist movement, and I hoped that a few days there might give me a flavor of that heady revolutionary environment.

I got off the train at the Jinggangshan Station fairly late one night. Hoping to find a taxi of some sort, I exited the station into a very dark western Jiangxi night. Four or five men who had been standing near cars and vans in a dirt parking lot approached me as I descended the steps from the station. I remember a light bulb hanging from a wire behind them. "I'll take you to Jinggangshan," one of them said, in a voice that made me fear for my safety for the first time since arriving in the PRC. "Take me *to* Jinggangshan?" I asked. "I thought this *was* Jinggangshan." Had I somehow gotten off the train at the wrong place?

No, but this was the Jinggangshan *station*, I learned from the group. It was four hours by mountain road from here to Jinggangshan *town*.

Those charmless fellows seemed way too excited by my vulnerability. I had no confidence that they would get me safely to the Maoist mecca. As I turned and walked back into the train station, they just laughed and called out: "*Those* guys are not going to take you to Jinggangshan!"

Back in the station, I found a man with a sympathetic face and explained my predicament. He saw my point and took me into a back room, where we were joined by a couple of higher-ups who began a polite but thorough interrogation. More and more of their railway colleagues came to observe the spectacle. Jinggangshan may have been four hours away, but I was touched by the spirit. Why had I come to this area? "I came to study the revolutionary spirit of Jinggangshan," I answered, thrilled that I was getting to talk like this in real life. "Yes, we have a Communist Party in the U.S., too," I remember answering another query.

They were a kind and professional group, tolerant of my cultural appropriation. Once they were satisfied that I was there for justifiable reasons, they told me that I could spend the night in the station dormitory; there was an extra bed. That message brought me one of the greatest feelings of relief I have ever had. Could something like this have happened at a small country Amtrak station? I don't think so. Maybe there was something to this revolutionary spirit after all.

The next morning, after delivering heartfelt thank-yous, I rode in a respectable county minibus to the town of Jinggangshan. I instantly fell in love with the place. The people really did seem friendlier and the cuisine fresher—both spicier and less greasy—than elsewhere. The air was clean, and a walk into the pine groves revealed red soil like that of the Sierras back home. I spent several days in the charming town, seeing the revolutionary sites and having pleasant conversations with restaurateurs and merchants. I made some purchases of soda pop, magazines, and other sundries at a small stand owned by a tiny elderly man with thick glasses. On Christmas Eve, I purchased a ticket for a 6:00 a.m. ride to Ganzhou the next day. But how would I wake up on time? Luckily, that favorite stand keeper of mine had stocked some cheap alarm clocks. I shudder to imagine why, but I must have hesitated at whatever terribly low price he quoted. The quick-thinking merchant came up with a solution: for four *yuan* he could offer a one-night *rental* of a small yellow clock.

As we were closing this deal, a couple of young men with whom I had chatted earlier came by the stand. It's your last night here in Jinggangshan, they insisted—so you've got to come drink with us. How could I say no? I followed them to their friend's business, a barbershop with sofas and mirrors across the back wall near the stairway. Mirrors, seating—pretty standard for a barbershop. But stairs? Hmmm. Eventually the counterrevolutionary reality of the one-young-woman-and-one-young-man traffic up and down the stairs dawned on me.

On to Ganzhou. It lacked Jinggangshan's reputation as a revolutionary base, yet I came to think of this dilapidated city as the most "Communist" place I visited during my time in China. I have photographs, taken right after I got off the bus, of Professor Zeng Biao and me drinking tea in an austere lounge. I am seated on a low couch, my backpack next to me, wearing a thick work shirt and high-waisted jeans. Professor Zeng, in a dark blazer over a dark sweater, nails the look that I loved so much in PRC academe at the time. He is smiling, but seems also to feel awkward—and that's how it feels in my memory, too. The man taking the photos was the Communist Party secretary in the history department. I have forgotten his name, but he shadowed Zeng and me for almost my whole visit.

In 1996 in Ganzhou, the CCP was still worried about what a professor might let an American know about a 1933 Youth Day track meet in the hills of the Jiangxi Soviet! I felt sad that a hardworking, generous, and decent man, as Professor Zeng showed himself to be, had to answer to a Party hack like this. I felt worse when I realized that he might even have to pay a price for my visit. My exercise of Western academic privilege might have created real trouble for him.

To be honest, though, I didn't have these guilt feelings until later. At the time, all I noticed was the very interesting visit that Professor Zeng and his minder were providing. It included, for example, the only ride I have ever had in an old Red Flag limo. (That's an example of what I mean by Gannan Normal being a most "Communist" place.) The three of us were driven to lunch at a small but clean restaurant close to campus. Everything there was spicy, with lots of peppers and black bean sauce in play, and my hosts cheerfully accommodated my vegetarian diet.

The most memorable touch, though, was a bottle of bitter gourd sorghum wine that our minder proudly brought to the table. "Look," he exulted, "there's a whole bitter gourd (*kugua*) inside this bottle of wine. All you do is take your chopsticks and . . ." Through the mouth of the bottle, he poked and jabbed and churned with his chopsticks until, about two minutes later, we had a bottle of fiery sorghum wine filled with chunks of pulp of bitter gourd. We got hammered.

Afterward, Professor Zeng took me around the city, and at some point our political minder left us alone. I have photos of us together at the Ganzhou Confucian Temple. The sorghum wine was catching up with me at that point, but the next part of the tour woke me up. Professor Zeng found two men who had turned their motorcycles into private taxis; the rest of our city tour was from that vantage point. My driver wore a helmet, but did not have one to offer me. I decided not to begrudge him this choice when he told me that he worked in an automobile factory where he was paid 250 *yuan*, or about US$30, monthly. My naïve question about why he wasn't at work brought a quick and logical answer: he and his companion had stepped out for a while to make some real money. Was this "Communist" or what?!

悟

A NIGHT AT THE MOVENPICK

Perry Link

1996

On the evening of July 8, 1996, I arrived at Beijing Capital Airport after a long, two-leg flight from Newark, New Jersey. I was coming to Beijing to give a lecture and to meet students and faculty in the Princeton-in-Beijing summer language program, of which I was a co-director. Friends from Princeton-in-Beijing were waiting for me outside the airport. In those days, the Beijing airport still bore some of the quaint flavor of the Mao era: drab walls, ceiling fans, luggage carousels built of wooden slats. The spanking-new construction that came with the city's hosting of the 2008 Summer Olympics was still in the future.

Passport control did have new computers, though, and when my turn in line came, a young officer squinted at his monitor, rather longer than one would think he had to, and then told me in halting English to take a seat and "wait a moment." About an hour later, another uniformed man, middle-aged with a long, serious face, returned to say, in Chinese (research on me done during the hour apparently had revealed that I could speak Chinese), that "we have checked with our superiors and you are not welcome in our country." I pointed out that I had a double-entry Chinese visa and asked what the problem was. He said nothing. He pointed an index finger upward and fixed me with a look.

I had arrived on a late flight, and there were no return flights to the United States until the next morning. This made me a problem for him and his colleagues, whose need to figure out where to put me over-night can explain at least part of my hour-long wait. In the end, four young plainclothes policemen accompanied me to the United Airlines ticket counter. One of them, with a crew cut and bushy eyebrows, was the leader. He told the United agent on duty that the airline had brought into China a passenger whose papers were unacceptable and said that the airline would need to provide a hotel room for one night. United, apparently preferring a minor expense to involvement in a visa dispute, paid for a room at the nearby, and very upscale, Moven-pick Hotel, and the four young policemen and I went there to spend the night. Officially, I had not entered China.

The young policemen smoked, and I do not, but other than that, I suffered no mistreatment. As I was brushing my teeth, the bushy-browed leader read to me in English the formal police language that it was his duty to read: "You cannot leave our company, you cannot make a phone call, you cannot . . ." and so on—about eight items in all. I just nodded my head, accepting everything. The phone call rule was especially relevant because, moments earlier, my only request had been to call my friends who were waiting for me outside the airport. I wanted to tell them to go home and not to worry. But the leader said this was not permitted and, to emphasize the point, had his colleagues unplug the telephone in the room and place it beneath the pillows on one of the beds.

After the official rules had been read, the speech of the four young policemen shifted to an informal register. They appeared to be ordi-nary young men, working for the police on as-needed assignment. We spoke in Chinese, which seemed to relax them. They expressed puzzlement that my Chinese tones were correct ("How did *that* hap-pen?" "Is your wife Chinese?") and then moved on to questions like how much my watch cost. They were glad to be with me in the Mov-enpick because the police system provides meal coupons for special-assignment work, so tonight they had a special opportunity to eat in the fancy restaurant on the ground floor. It was past 11:00 p.m., but never mind; they wanted dinner. One suddenly turned to me.

"You must be hungry!"

"No," I said, "I'm not."

"Come on, let's eat!" Rule One said that I could not leave their com-pany. That meant, too, that they could not leave mine.

"I'm not hungry." Truly I was not; I just wanted to sleep. An awkward pause ensued.

"We have coupons!" Another awkward pause.

"Do you have one for me?" I knew that they didn't, of course. I was just teasing.

"Uh . . . no sir, we don't." *Xiansheng* (sir) marked a clear descent from the gruff officialese they had used when reading the rules to me.

"Then what can I eat?" I continued my teasing.

"You . . . you can pay your own way."

I still refused. They consulted and decided to take turns. Three of them went down to eat, while one, smoking and chatting, stayed with me. When the three came back, the one went down.

The next morning they took me back to the airport and to the United counter for check-in.

"The flight is full," said the agent.

"If this passenger is not on the flight, the airplane will not leave the airport," the leader said. I doubt that this was an idle threat. In any case, United did find me a seat, and I headed back to Newark. The cabin crew, who were the same as those who had flown in the day before, expressed surprise that I had finished my work in China so quickly.

OPIUM WAR

Andrew D. Morris

1996

I took it as a compliment until I realized how unimpressive the competition was. He Yan, an actor and director living in Hangzhou, had approached the director of Foreign Affairs at Hangzhou University. He was assistant director on a film project and needed someone—a white man who could speak Chinese—to play the part of a translator. He found me. He was asking me to be in a movie directed by the famous director Xie Jin! All very exciting, until I realized that I was almost literally the only person on campus who met the two criteria.

I was told to meet two actors at the Hangzhou train station; they would escort me to Dinghai, on the coast, about 135 miles away. One of the actors was a charming rogue named Mr. Yang Zhaoquan, a born performer and master of witty stories. The other was a quiet, soulful man named Li Weixin, who became my roommate at the People's Liberation Army Unit 37502 No. 1 Hostel in Dinghai. His acting role was to be the patriotic Magistrate Deng Tingzhen, and he did it beautifully.

On our first night in Dinghai, the city hosted a large variety show to honor famed director Xie and the 155th anniversary of a battle against the British. I jotted down notes that night on some of the performances: a reenactment of the brave Chinese defense at Dinghai; a *xiangsheng* comedians' dialogue piece by the actors Yang and Li; a male dance team wearing matching sleeveless camo tops and camo shorts, red berets, and long black socks. Xie Jin spoke briefly to the crowd on what he saw as the main theme of the war and of his film: *luohou jiu yao aida*, a jingoistic adage that translates uncomfortably as "the backward will always be beaten." Oh, so it was going to be *that* kind of movie.

That same night, I was summoned to Xie's hotel room to meet him. He was chewing on something the whole three minutes I was in his room and asked me a question that, through the chewing, I could not understand. When I hesitated to answer, an assistant director, who would soon earn the disdain of most of the cast as Xie's "running dog," snarled at me, "He asked you a question." Oh, it was going to be *that* kind of crew.

The next day, I was taken to the makeup department, whose job it was to make me look properly British, foreign, and white. My dark, wavy hair wouldn't do; before I knew it they had made me into, as I expressed it in my notes, a "permed blonde dipshit." (I did save a crumb of dignity by refusing to let them bleach my eyebrows.)

I had to find a hat to cover up this disaster. The only ones I could find in town were the old blue "socialist" caps, but the cashier said, "Those are for old people," and couldn't believe I wanted one. It didn't matter; they were all too small anyway.

I met several of the British actors, including Oliver Cotton, a famed Shakespearean actor who was in all three of the scenes I was in, and who struck me as one of the most urbane, intelligent, and impressive people I had ever met. I earned his trust when I interpreted for him in the makeup department, where together we avoided the mutton-chops that they had seen in a book on Engels and had in mind for him. Things got even more interesting when I met some of the dozens of extras who had been shipped from Xinjiang to play British soldiers and sailors. I knew I was in new territory when a tall light-skinned redhead sized me up and asked, in Chinese, "Are you Chinese?" He was Russian. Most of the others that I spent time with, drinking and listening to them speak bitterness, were Uzbeks and Uyghurs. They did not look British, and they knew it. But after years of being called *laowai* ("foreigners"), they enjoyed getting the best of this exchange: 300 *yuan* (US$36) a day to pretend they were stabbing Han Chinese.

The next day, we went out to the replica British ship to rehearse. A pretty young actress from Sichuan sat down next to me and asked if I could help her translate some Michael Bolton lyrics. I also got to know Naren Hua, the beautiful Mongolian actress who lived in London and Hong Kong and was serving as another assistant director for the film. (The crew and cast called her, incorrectly and Han-chauvinistically, "Sister Na.") She advised me on how to prepare for my acting debut as the British naval translator John Robert Morrison. She saw Morrison—like her, like me—as straddling two languages and cultures.

My main scene was a negotiation on the ship between the characters played by Oliver Cotton and Li Weixin. This was intimidating. These two actors were such pros, gesturing and summoning vocal inflections that brought the shameful confrontation of 1842 vividly back to life. I had several lines in Chinese and in English as my character, Morrison, tried his best to bridge the two very different worldviews. I won praise from Naren Hua when I corrected a mispronounced character. But fans of my work on screen will likely know me best for a line that I mutter, in orientalist frustration, to the captain played by Cotton: "This is so typically Chinese; they never say yes and they never say no."

It was a clever line written to illustrate the less clever point about being backward and bullied. On screen, it helps the captain to decide to start his attack, and we see a "British" (Uzbek, actually) gunner declare "Prepare to fire" in what can only be described as less than the Queen's English. But his mangling of the three words was not due to our lack of trying. He had listened to me saying the phrase over and over, had transcribed the sounds into Uzbek script, and had done his best.

One of my shorter scenes was filmed in a tent at night. I was to enter the scene on a certain beat, but that unpopular assistant director kept changing it. When I failed on the third or fourth take, he snapped at me, and I snapped back. I told him to make up his mind. The crew gasped, and I knew immediately I had overstepped my bounds. Ms. Naren, who had been so supportive earlier, came to me later with a rebuke. I felt embarrassed, exhausted, and out of my element. I was looking forward to getting back to Hangzhou. When Xie got word of this, he lived up to his favorite adage. He told me that I had thin hands like a girl. He had shot that tent scene so that I would appear on screen for the shortest possible time and in a focus softer than a little girl's hands. Most nastily of all, the film's end credits did not include my name (or Morrison's). Those with power will always use it. The backward will always be beaten.

I learned a lot about filmmaking during those days and have never watched another movie the same way since. I was paid 300 *yuan* per day, the same as the other "foreign" comrades from Xinjiang. The sweetest reward, though, came the next summer when the film was released. My wife and I went to see it in Hangzhou alongside the crowds who had received free tickets from school or their workplace to view this "patriotic education" film. After my big scene, the middle-aged man in front of me turned to his wife and whispered, "Hey, that foreigner speaks good Chinese!"

SPECIAL POWERS

Jeremy Brown

1997

I had a surprising amount of spare time in Harbin in spring 1997, when I was a nineteen-year-old sophomore on my first extended trip outside the United States. My main task in Harbin was to study Chinese, but my teachers there assumed that characters and tones were too difficult for foreigners to learn properly, so they assigned very little homework and didn't bother correcting me when I mispronounced tones. I had an especially hard time with the third tone–second tone combination, which I had to use several times a day when people asked me where I was from. I always responded, "I have no nuts" (*méi guŏrén*). Everyone knew that I was trying to say I was American (*Mĕiguórén*), but nobody told me that I was butchering things.

At college in Oregon, my days had been full of studying, running cross-country, and practicing piano. In Harbin, my academic load was light and my extracurricular hours were wide open. I discovered the existence of a single piano, but it was behind a curtain in the main university auditorium. The custodian allowed me to touch it only once every other week. Playing piano so infrequently was more painful than not playing at all, so I gave it up. I also tried to join the Harbin Institute of Technology long-distance running team, but the runs were frigid and treacherous outings on the black ice of city streets. For hours after each effort I coughed up coal dust. I quit after a week.

Unable to do the things that had given my life meaning as a teenager in the United States, I ended up wandering around Harbin on foot for hours every week. I spent a lot of time in one Xinhua Bookstore, trying to figure out which books might help me understand China. Occasionally I bought books, including a novel titled *Hot Dog*, as well as the popular anti-American screed *China Can Say No*.

I didn't learn much about China from these books. I spent more time looking up unfamiliar characters in my dictionary than I did on *Hot Dog*. But I did keep returning to the store. One day when I was browsing the shelves, a young man in his twenties stood next to me for a minute or two. Finally he blurted out, "I know a girl who has *teneng*. Would you like to meet her?" I said, "What's *teneng*?" I didn't fully understand the man's response, but he was gesturing to his forehead and saying something about a third eye, which he called a *tianmu*. This sounded more interesting than *Hot Dog*, and I didn't have anything better to do, so I said yes, I wanted to meet the *teneng* girl. My new friend, whose name was Song, said he would take me to see her the next night.

When I got back to my room at the PLA-run hotel where the American students in Harbin lived, I told my Chinese roommate Hongyu that I was going to meet someone who had *teneng*. I couldn't find the word in my dictionary and asked him to explain it to me. Hongyu, a Communist Party member a few months away from receiving his PhD in engineering, was six years older than I. He laughed nervously.

"It means special powers, supernatural powers, like seeing through walls," he said. "It's superstitious."

The next evening, Song and I got on a bus. Song kept putting his hand on my knee and palpating rhythmically, as if he were squeezing a melon at the market. We arrived at a gated apartment complex and met Wei, the *teneng* girl, and her father, who worked at a machine-gun factory. We started with small talk ("I have no nuts"), tea, and salted melon seeds. Wei's dad, nervous and excited to meet a foreigner, asked me if I was a spy and joked that the threat of America's powerful army was keeping his factory in business. He chain-smoked and jiggled his legs furiously. His daughter was quiet and calm. "Did you bring any pictures of your family?" Wei asked me. I hadn't. "Do you have any samples of your relatives' handwriting?" I didn't. "That's going to make it a lot harder, but I'll try anyway."

Wei closed her eyes. Thirty seconds passed. She opened her eyes and said, "Your mother is watching television." What a joke, I thought. My mom had thrown out our TV when I was in high school because my sister and I were spending hours a day in front of the screen. My mother didn't have a television. Wei closed her eyes again, this time for a full minute. Then she looked straight at me and said, "Your father." I scoffed, more certain than ever that Wei was about to reveal herself as a fraud. My father had died of a heart attack a week after my second birthday. I had no memory of him, but growing up I was keenly aware of his absence. Wei continued, "Your father. Your father just wants to say that he misses you very much." I was stunned. My skepticism melted away. If Wei had said that my father was watching a movie, I would have laughed. Instead she said what I truly wanted to hear. I choked up and asked Wei to tell my father that I missed him too. Song squeezed my leg again on the bus back to the PLA hotel.

In addition to having the privilege of sharing a large hotel room instead of living with three other PhD students in a squalid dormitory, my roommate Hongyu was one of the few people in Harbin in 1997 who had access to a computer connected to the Internet. Once a week he let me into the engineering computer lab to check my email. The next chance I got, I wrote to my mom and asked if she had watched TV recently. I didn't explain why. When I returned to the lab and read her response, I learned that at the moment Wei had opened her third eye, my mother had been at a friend's house watching *Mystery!* on PBS.

I don't know if Wei was a Falun Gong practitioner or a follower of one of the many other *qigong* sects that proliferated in China during the 1990s. The words "Falun Gong" did not appear in *People's Daily* or the *New York Times* until 1999, when in April a massive demonstration by more than 10,000 followers outside Zhongnanhai in Beijing shocked China's top leaders and prompted them to ban Falun Gong's self-cultivation exercises three months later. In Harbin in 1997, I never heard the term "Falun Gong," never saw Wei again, and spent the rest of the semester trying to avoid Song, who kept showing up unannounced at my door and whose strangeness caused my roommate and the security guard downstairs to recoil. I didn't mind his weirdness, but the knee squeezing made me uncomfortable.

Nowadays, as a professor in Canada, I give an annual lecture about Falun Gong to undergraduates, many of whom grew up in China during the 2000s, when propaganda demonized the religious sect as an evil cult. When I mention Falun Gong practitioners' purported supernatural powers, including opening the "heavenly eye," students from China guffaw. One time a male student shouted "bullshit," garnering even more laughs. They quiet down, however, when I tell them about Wei's *teneng*. I was certainly not part of any *qigong* group's target demographic in 1997, but I understood the appeal. Wei knew precisely what to say to an aimless American who kept telling strangers that he had no nuts and who missed his parents more than he realized. I'd say that she had special powers.

悟

RELATIONSHIPS, NOT NAMES

David Moser

1998

I was teaching at the Beijing Foreign Studies University in the late 1990s, and my daughter Leah (Chinese name Li Mo) spent her preschool years on that campus, playing in the compound with the local children. When she was about three, her best friends were a boy called Doudou and a girl called Lele, and the three of them soon became inseparable playmates. As a result, my wife, Lihua, and I naturally ended up spending some time with the two sets of parents, chatting while the kids played in the yard, celebrating birthdays together, and going on outings to the zoo or the shopping mall. We were by no means close friends, but when your kids are chummy, you get to know the parents.

After about two years, I got another job, and before moving out of the foreign experts building, we wanted to give a good-bye gift to the parents of Doudou and Lele. I had the gifts wrapped, and was preparing to write a message on the cards, when I suddenly realized I didn't know the names of Doudou's and Lele's parents, not even their surnames. This seemed a bit odd, but I figured this was a result of my nonnative listening comprehension. Surely my wife, a native Chinese speaker, would have picked up the names of the two sets of parents by now. But when I asked her, she simply shrugged and said, "I don't know either. I guess I just never asked them."

How could it be that neither of us knew any of the names of the two couples we had known and interacted with for two years? Looking back, I realized that this state of affairs was the outcome of a long-recognized cultural difference. In social interactions at all levels of Chinese society, terms of address focus on the relationships between the participants, and not the other person's individual identity. Whereas in an English context, casual acquaintances will quickly exchange names—indeed, it would be awkward not to do so—in the Chinese context, it is customary to address the other person in a way that reaffirms their role or direct relationship in the situation. Thus, for example, when Doudou's mother phoned me, the conversation would begin, "Is this Momo's father? This is Doudou's mother. Would Momo like to go to the park with us today?" Upon which I would report to my wife that "Doudou's mother just called and asked if Momo wants to go to the park," and so on. In English, we are all individuals; in Chinese we are nodes in a web of relationships.

悟

ESTRANGEMENT

Nick Admussen

1999

In 1999 there were two little stores across from the foreign-student dormitory at Nanjing University, where I was studying Chinese. They were right next to each other and basically identical: they sold soft drinks, cigarettes, instant noodles, toilet paper, alcohol, and a small array of plastic goods. As with identical enterprises generally, the two competed fiercely. I favored the store on the left because the woman who ran it was patient with my bad Chinese. My friend Mike favored the store on the right because its owner would bring out a flattened cardboard box upon which Mike could sit as he enjoyed a beverage on the store's front steps.

I am not, however, the most reliable ally to small businesses. As my Chinese improved and I could navigate the gruffer proprietor on the right, I was lured away by the prospect of my own box chair, as well as by the low-tar Zhongnanhai-light cigarettes that had begun appearing in his right-hand display case (as if the difference between five and ten *ke* of tar per cigarette would somehow better protect my health). Mine was but a small betrayal, but I felt guilty about it, and it became hard to meet the eyes of the folks at the left-hand store. We students lived in a huge high-rise full of foreigners, and our local friends were mostly college students. I longed to meet some regular people, outside of university life, and now I'd burned my most consistent daily relationship just for a few grams of tar.

One night (which I hope was on a weekend) we were drinking Jinling beer in front of the right-hand store when the boss of the left-hand store left her counter and squatted down next to me. She handed me a hundred-page bilingual instruction manual for a certain device that she said belonged to her father—and now was not working. She wanted my help. I was, at the time, about halfway through a third-year Chinese-language course that included lessons like "Welcoming the Spring Festival" and "The Lives of Overseas Chinese." I struggled to hear and reproduce the words I needed day to day, like *Jiādélè* (Gatorade, as I didn't yet have the habit of drinking tea) or *miànjīnzhǐ* (facial tissue, which was endlessly useful). And now I was holding what, upon examination, was a set of technical specifications and warnings for a human pacemaker.

"Your father has this . . . inside his chest?" *Yes.* "How do you know it doesn't work?" *His heart stops sometimes.* "You need to see the doctor." *It's expensive.* "This side is in Chinese—you can read it." *I don't read well, it's a foreign machine, can you tell me why it's not working?*

My first impulse, which now embarrasses me, was to think that this was some sort of elaborate ruse to create a personal connection that would entice me to move my business back to the left-hand store. I was, after all, far from the most bilingual foreigner that visited the shops, and self-evidently was no scientist. I was also three-quarters of the way through a 600-milliliter beer—so why *me*, for Christ's sake? My second impulse was to imagine that Chinese people must think that all foreigners are secret technologists, highly educated, and wickedly ingenious. Both these reactions faded, mercifully, as quickly as they came.

What persisted was an unshakable sense that no matter what I learned or what I could do while living in China, I was and would remain a stranger, full stop. Over the years to come, the way I was seen would depend mostly on the person who was looking: I was cast as a genius, a naïve child, an ally, an enemy. There were also, I found, many Chinese who not only tolerated my estrangement but recognized it as similar to their own. Many of the people around me felt rightly estranged from mainstream Chinese culture. Speaking mostly dialect, reading just a hundred or so characters, alternately treated as invisible or expendable, it shouldn't have been surprising that the left-hand shop owner felt she was living in a world that made more sense to me than it did to her, or that she reached out to one of the vagabond-looking foreigners on the street. After all, we had something in common: devices in our chests that came from far away.

Part VII

悟

Today's Everyday

In the early twenty-first century, the Chinese economy continued its un-precedented growth and, in 2016, became the second largest in the world. Beijing took a far more active role in asserting territorial claims in the East Asian region and in cultivating economic ties around the world. The Beijing Summer Olympics of 2008 were touted as a crowning achievement, but it was also in 2008 that a national scandal over tainted baby formula emerged and a devastating earthquake took nearly seventy thousand lives in Sichuan because of, in part, shoddy construction of schools and other buildings whose inferior quality was widely viewed to be the result of poor regulation and outright corruption. As Western scholars observed these triumphs and trag-edies in the news, in quieter corners they were also enjoying increased access to more remote parts of China and to national, provincial, and local archives. Access to border regions and marginalized people became more possible than in earlier years.

悟

LIVING IN THE WHITE HOUSE

Marketus D. Presswood

2000

In 2000, I had just moved back to China from Japan and was job hunting, so I needed to find a cheap place to live on a tight budget. My housing search ended when I found a place called "The White House" (*baigong*). It was the beginning of the period in which Chinese real estate developers began borrowing the names of famous Western properties and districts for their projects. "SOHO" and "Central Park" appeared in the new Chinese twenty-first-century urban landscape. The White House, located in Haidian District in northwest Beijing, was a two-story building that was laid out like a traditional rectangular *siheyuan* courtyard stacked one on top of another. You entered a lobby that was facing the west and opened to a center quad with individual dorm rooms on three sides with windows facing the inner courtyard. The complex was situated down a small nondescript alley off Qinghua Road that was almost impossible to see at night. Pedestrians disappeared into the shadows of this backstreet. Most of the tenants were students from Japan, Korea, and Southeast Asia. An attraction of the White House was that it allowed tenants to pay monthly without a long-term commitment. At least that is what my English contract said.

A couple of months after I moved in, I found a job working for the Canadian embassy in Beijing. My new office was in the Chaoyang district, quite far from Haidian. A move was essential. I found a new apartment and recruited my new coworker, Amanda, a Chinese-Canadian, and another friend to help me get my stuff out of my old apartment to the new one. After work, we set off in Amanda's cool SUV. Once we got to my room, we began moving my stuff into her car. I informed the person at the front desk that I was leaving—my rent for the month had already been paid in full. It was my understanding that I was free to move out at any time if I did not owe them any money—which I didn't.

The concierge appeared nonplussed and nervous. She quickly began fumbling through files. I continued to load the car.

"You cannot leave!" I heard the young woman say. "You have only stayed here two months!" I politely informed her that my contract stated that I could leave when I wanted and that I was current with my rent. "You must stay for four months!" she exclaimed. "You owe us two months' rent!" Now I was confused. Just two months ago this same woman had told me that I was not obligated to stay for a fixed term. I did not have time or the desire to deal with this and just got into Amanda's SUV to drive away. I was not going to be shaken down for extra money. As we drove off down the dark alley and reached the main road, we heard a huge thump on the roof. To our surprise, two of the doormen had jumped on the roof of the SUV.

"Naaaahhh!!!! They can't be that desperate," I said to Amanda. "They are going to jump off any second now . . ." Nope! A moment later, a car filled with young Chinese guys drove next to our vehicle and asked the two guys on top of the car if they needed any help. At this point, this situation just seemed so surreal. Amanda was getting scared, and I told her to turn around and take these guys back to the White House. When we returned, the owner was waiting for us in the lobby. We immediately got into an argument about what I thought was an unscrupulous business practice of "bait and switch." After an hour of fruitless dialogue, I threw my hands in the air in palpable frustration and let out a huge sigh: "Fuuuccckk!"

"*Bie ma ren!*" (Don't curse at people!) the owner shouted.

"I didn't direct my curse at you," I retorted.

He then turned his ire at Amanda. "*Ni shi Zhongguoren! Ni yinggai bangzhu Zhongguoren!*" (You are Chinese! You should be helping Chinese people!)

"Fuck you! I'm Canadian!" Amanda shouted. The owner's face went red. Meanwhile, to our surprise, a white van had pulled up outside the glass lobby door, and out came about ten shirtless Chinese men with sticks and chains. The situation had just gone from zero to sixty in three seconds.

"Where are you from!?" the owner kept asking me. I told him I was American, but he obviously did not believe me. "Where's your passport!?" he demanded. "You are African!" I did not have my passport because my visa was being renewed. This was a moment in my life when I really needed my American identity. I also felt self-conscious that I had to play that card at the expense of my African heritage. I showed the owner my work ID from the Canadian embassy, but that didn't satisfy him. I could see in Amanda's eyes that she was becoming more frightened. I needed to resolve this situation ASAP!

I called the local Chinese police, and they arrived in about ten minutes. The lead officer, after hearing both of our explanations, told the owner to let me go. He knew the owner was trying to swindle me. We were about to be allowed to leave! Thank God! I thought. Then the owner motioned for the officer to accompany him to his office to have a private chat. After ten minutes, the police officer and the owner reemerged. The policeman sat on a sofa near me and simply told me, "You handle the situation."

What had just happened!? The owner was in full control again and he became even more arrogant. "You must pay two months' rent and apologize to my staff!" I looked pleadingly at the officer. His expression told me, "You are on your own, I've been paid." Out of fear and concern, not just for myself, but my friends, I acquiesced. I grudgingly paid the money and made the apologies. We got in the car and drove off. My brief stay in the White House was behind me. I never looked back.

悟

THE LOUDNESS OF THE LAMBS

Dru C. Gladney

2003–2004

In 2003–2004, I was allowed to travel high up into the Altai mountains near Xinjiang's border with Mongolia to visit nomadic Kazakh herders. I traveled with two companions, or minders: a middle-aged Kazakh official with ties to the nomadic families, and a Han official from Urumqi who was responsible for me while in Xinjiang.

We took the first of many trips together, leaving by jeep from the Fuyun county seat of the Altai Mountain District. We drove for six hours on a paved road to Keketuohai town, then on a dirt road for three more hours to a base camp made up of a few large Kazakh tents. Our first visit was in late March on a lovely spring day with rushing streams and verdant pastures. After several days there, the Kazakh official negotiated horses and provisions for us to ride up into the mountains. The region tightly restricted outside visitors, mostly in order to prevent illegal logging or mining, so we knew that we would encounter only the occasional Kazakh herding group.

Leaving the base camp, it took us about eight hours of riding to find the first Kazakh encampment of three to six tents (*ger* or yurts). Families camped there for a day or two during their seasonal migrations up to higher summer pastures. That afternoon, we were welcomed in the tents and treated to some leftovers of stewed lamb, cold noodles, hard cheeses, and naan bread. After staying the night, we left at the break of day with the herders, who were eager to move up into the higher elevations and more fertile pastures for their mixed herds of sheep, goats, cows, horses, and camels.

On the second day, after several more hours of fairly hard riding with only a short break for tea, hard cheese, and bread crusts, the Han official complained of acute saddle sores and turned back to the base camp, leaving me and the Kazakh official to continue to travel with the herders. My Kazakh minder was keen for me to visit as many camps as I could in order to gain a better understanding of the time-honored herding techniques and the extended-family structures of the people. It was his responsibility to check on how the families were doing. He also anticipated the rich hospitality that he knew would be coming our way.

By mid-morning, we approached another Kazakh camp. A young boy spotted us and galloped back to the main camp to tell the elders that we were coming. As we drew nearer, I heard the bleating of the sheep, which grew louder as we were welcomed into one of the main tents and offered tea and snacks. The noise from the sheep continued as we talked. It reached a crescendo and then—abruptly—stopped. After an hour or so, our host told us that a lamb had been slaughtered in our honor and asked us to stay for a long lunch of special Kazakh fare.

After several similar rides into the mountains with my minders, and more visits to these small Kazakh encampments, this welcoming with the chorus of sheep followed by the feast of stewed lamb became a pattern. Once I made an excuse to leave the tent while the sheep were still crying out. I discovered that while we were inside with our tea, one of the herders was among the flock choosing which lamb would be slaughtered. The lambs had turned to form a small circle, facing inward and crying loudly. The older sheep had surrounded them, to all appearances trying to protect them. The herder waded in among them and selected one unfortunate lamb, then took it aside and dealt with it according to religiously prescribed rituals. As soon as the lamb was slaughtered, the sheep stopped their crying and an abrupt and rather eerie quiet descended. After my discovery, that strange stillness kept me from enjoying the feast that followed, despite the warm welcome and heartfelt generosity of our Kazakh hosts.

After many long days on horseback navigating steep and difficult terrain, this pattern became the hardest part of the trip. Eventually, I persuaded my Kazakh minder to avoid arriving at camps before the midday meal. If we arrived in the late afternoon, we would be welcomed with meats, raisins, cheese, bread, and milk tea—all delicious—but not fresh lamb. My Kazakh minder could never understand why I didn't appreciate the sacrifice and generosity of the herders, since they all knew we both loved Kazakh food.

MEN'S WORLD

Jeremy Brown

2004

I tried in vain to persuade the staff at the Tianjin Municipal Archive to show me interesting and useful documents in 2004. I bantered in Tianjin dialect. I played table tennis with staff at lunch. I squeegeed windows to prepare for the National Day holiday. Nothing worked. I wanted colorful human stories of rural people coming to the city and urbanites spending time in the countryside, but all the archivists would give me were boring statistical reports. Some weeks they gave me nothing at all. The good news was that I was getting so skilled at Ping-Pong that the archive workers started calling me "Little Wa," after Jan-Ove Waldner, the Swedish Olympic medalist in table tennis and the only white guy who came close to threatening Chinese dominance in the sport. The bad news was that my dissertation research was a disaster.

Desperate, I started spending less time at the archive and more time at the flea market, where a tight-knit group of middle-aged men who had been laid off as factory workers or truck drivers made a meager living selling used books and discarded documents. Highly literate and deeply cynical, the peddlers squatted on low wooden stools, smoking cheap cigarettes and talking up their wares. They welcomed me into their world. Where the official archive staff had been stiff and recalcitrant, the document peddlers went out of their way to be help-ful, trying to explain my project to one another and actively acquiring files they thought I might want to buy.

Lao Wang wore thick oversized Jiang Zemin–style glasses. He didn't possess many documents himself, but he became my protector and broker in the flea market, and he quickly understood my research focus even better than I did. On at least two Saturday mornings, Wang called me at home at 6:00 a.m. to make sure I would be coming to the market that day. Wang had a friend named Lao Mou. Mou had two teeth left in his mouth; two long strands of hair sprouted out of the top of his otherwise bald head. Mou was quieter than Wang, but he had access to a seemingly endless stream of interesting documents.

Two of my dissertation chapters grew directly out of my interac-tion with Wang, Mou, and other peddlers. If I had stayed put in the archive, I might have qualified for the Olympics in table tennis, but I never would have learned about how city officials had directed and funded the deportation of political enemies from Tianjin to villages during the Cultural Revolution. The peddlers, who knew that I was looking for anything related to city people going to the countryside, introduced me to files dealing with individual deportees as well as of-ficial policy documents. They also talked about their own experiences during the 1970s.

It was Lao Mou who first told me about 6985. It took me a while to figure out what he was talking about, but I learned that 6985 was the code name for a civil defense project that had broken ground in the Taihang Mountains of southwest Hebei province on August 5, 1969. Also known as the Tianjin Ironworks, 6985 aimed to establish a secure source of steel for Tianjin in the event that the Soviet Union or the United States were to bomb coastal China. The ironworks itself was a virtual island of city space in the middle of a remote rural hinterland. Thousands of Tianjin youth went to 6985 as construction laborers, miners, and factory workers. Many of them eventually returned to

Tianjin during the 1980s, and one of them, a friend of Mou's named Lao Tang, ended up selling documents in the flea market.

Tang regaled me with stories about the time he spent underground in the mines connected to 6985. He introduced me to a network of fellow displaced urbanites, encouraged me to travel to the site myself, and recommended a documentary about 6985 that had aired a few years earlier on Tianjin Television (TJTV). I wanted to see the documentary to prepare myself for fieldwork at the ironworks. The only way to watch it was to find the producer and to arrange a screening of the master tape inside the TJTV compound. My peddler friends could not get me into TJTV, but my academic contacts could. Producer Li welcomed me at the gate to the TJTV compound, took me into a dark room, and pressed play. I feverishly took notes and the stage was set for a mind-blowing research trip to the ironworks.

A few days after I returned to Tianjin from 6985, my phone rang. It was Producer Li, who was no longer making documentaries. He was working on a new talk show called *Men's World*. Could I come to the station the next day for the taping of two episodes? The first episode would be "Men Talk about Their Careers." The second was "Men Talk about Their Wives." After a few unpleasant experiences, I had sworn to myself that I would never again be a guest on TV in China, and—while I couldn't say this to Producer Li—I thought that *Men's World* was an awful idea for a TV show. As a self-identified feminist who was the only male in my household growing up (as a result, I vigilantly put down the toilet seat after peeing), I had no idea what I could contribute to a talk show about men's issues. Everywhere I looked, Chinese society itself was a men's world. Did men really need their own show? Producer Li's voice interrupted my train of thought: "Are you still there? Can you come?" My political stance was irrelevant. Li had gone out of his way to help me and I owed him a favor.

The next afternoon, I was sweating under the TJTV studio's klieg lights. "Men Talk about their Careers" went smoothly, but "Men Talk about their Wives" was raucous. The guests included an African exchange student who claimed he was a prince who had eight wives. I also shared the stage with a flamboyant Chinese novelist and a French man who answered a series of questions about romance. When I spoke, I tried to reconcile my belief that the institution of marriage perpetuated patriarchal oppression with my love for my wife (what I didn't add was that my longtime girlfriend and I had gotten married a year earlier in a failed attempt to get a spousal stipend added to my

Fulbright grant—but we did save fifty dollars on our car insurance). The show ended with each guest looking directly into the camera and conveying a heartfelt message to his wife. The French guest was better at this part than I was.

I moved on with my research, forgot about *Men's World*, and returned to California after a year that had been greatly enriched by the document peddlers' insights and yellowed papers. When I returned to Tianjin the following summer, one of my first stops was the flea market. The regulars were all there, including Wang, Tang, and Mou, who still had two teeth but who now had only one long hair coming out of his head. Wang and Tang did most of the talking, but as I got ready to leave, Mou said, "Hey, I saw you on *Men's World* a while back. You did great!" Incredulous, I didn't think to connect Mou teaching me about 6985 to the exchange of favors that led to my TV appearance. All I could say was, "Really? You watch that?" Mou replied, "It's my favorite. I watch it every week."

悟

MALLEABLE RULES

Philip F. Williams

2004

I was enjoying a successful book-buying and sightseeing excursion from Hong Kong to Shenzhen in June of 2004 when my passport was stolen in a melee of pimps. A tour-bus driver had dropped me off after dark on a Friday night, about half a mile from my hotel in a business district that looked much sleazier than it had earlier that day. Hustlers outside of nightclubs, hair salons, and massage parlors called out as I passed by, some going so far as to grab my shoulder and try to steer me indoors. Sometimes there were two hustlers jostling me at the same time, one in front and one in back. The only police officers I saw were shut safely inside an occasional kiosk in the median of the street, apparently uninterested in the antics of the aggressive pimps.

When I reached a restaurant near my hotel ten minutes later, I saw that the small front pocket of my backpack had been unzipped, and I was shocked to find my passport was gone. I walked to a local Public Security Bureau (PSB) office inside a parking structure and reported the theft. I would have to apply for a replacement passport at the nearest U.S. Consulate, in Guangzhou, and then apply for an exit visa at the PSB visa office in Guangzhou.

Besides buying books and seeing the sights of Shenzhen, I was slated to present two conference papers in Singapore in a matter of days. One of my two conference presentations was scheduled for Wednesday morning, and my Tuesday flight out of Hong Kong was nonrefundable.

After a late-night emergency call to the consulate, I took an early morning train there and was allowed to bypass a long line of Chinese visa applicants at the gate. The consular officers were extremely efficient and punctual, and before closing time that day, Saturday, they handed me my replacement passport. The PSB visa office would not open again until Monday, so I would have only that one business day to secure a PRC exit visa if I was to have any chance of making the Tuesday flight out of Hong Kong.

Monday morning, I packed, checked out of my hotel, and arrived at Guangzhou's PSB visa office just as their doors opened. When I reached the counter, I presented my passport and exit visa form to a bored-looking middle-aged clerk who said that my documents seemed to be in order. When I asked if I could please pick up my exit visa by closing time since I had a flight to catch the following morning, she let out a loud guffaw and blurted that every visa applicant should allow at least two or three business days for the visa to be issued. Trying to be as courteous as possible, I asked if it might be possible to pay an additional fee for one-day service. Her expression hardened and she shook her head no. I told her I would need to think more about the situation and asked her to return my passport and visa application. She seemed relieved to have washed her hands of a pesky foreigner.

I found a seat from which I could eye the row of clerks who were accepting visa applications, observing their demeanor as they dealt with applicants. Maybe another clerk would be more sympathetic. A young fellow who might have been a recent college graduate struck me as the most conscientious and efficient. I grabbed my papers and got into his line. After he accepted my application and passport, I explained my situation. He said that he would try his best and advised me to show up a half hour before closing time. I thanked him for his excellent care and left.

Ten minutes prior to closing time, the busy young clerk called me over to his window and handed me my passport with the exit visa inside. At the other end of the counter, the clerk who had scoffed at my request had long since stopped working and was reading her newspaper. But a weight had been lifted from my shoulders, and I thanked the busy man for his consideration and efficiency. Rules in China, I realized, were subject to individual interpretation even at this routine level, and kindness can always overcome cynicism, depending on the person.

悟

TASHKURGAN

Justin M. Jacobs

2007

The name of the town was Tashkurgan, and getting there proved more difficult than I had imagined.

I had already spent several days among the nomadic Kyrgyz, sleeping in their yurts and doing my best to dodge their camels, horses, and motorbikes. But the goal had always been to reach Tashkurgan—the last stop on the road from China to Pakistan. I wanted to go just so that I could say that I'd been there. Urumchi, the capital of Xinjiang—the far northwestern "Uyghur Autonomous Region" of China—simply wasn't enough. Nor were the teeming bazaars of Kashgar or the distant southern oases of the Taklamakan Desert.

I really needed to go to Tashkurgan. I simply wouldn't be satisfied until I had gone as far west as I could possibly go in China. Then I would turn right back around and retrace my steps. I desperately needed that notch on my belt. Back in the day, scholars of China could get all the credibility they needed just by making it to Beijing or Shanghai. Heck, even Taiwan or Hong Kong would do. But times had changed, and the bar had risen considerably. Tashkurgan could help me reach it.

To get there, you take the Karakorum Highway. It's a lonely place. You can stand by the side of the road for hours without a single vehicle passing by. On this particular day, standing a stone's throw away from the icy blue waters of Karakul Lake, the drivers of those vehicles that did rumble through apparently had no interest in stopping for an unshaven backpacker in cocky Aviator sunglasses.

Finally, a Kyrgyz shepherd managed to flag down a truck, telling me to hide behind a rock while he negotiated a fare. "If he sees you," he said, "he will double the price." For the next three hours, I was hitching my way to the last outpost of Chinese empires of yore.

How cool would that sound in my next e-mail home?!

The truck's driver and his sidekick somehow reminded me of the odd-couple contract killers who stole the show in the dark comedy *Fargo*. One was chatty and funny looking and seemed harmless enough, jabbering away about this and that. But his brooding companion in the back looked like he could hardly wait to get his hands on an axe and a wood chipper. I had never hitched a ride in my life and was none too comfortable doing so here at the ends of the earth. For the next three hours, I couldn't help but wonder what a blade between my shoulders might feel like.

Of course, knives are ubiquitous in Xinjiang. Grown Uyghur men, especially those from rural areas, often carry one on their belts. I did a double take the first time I spotted one. It was tucked in the waistband of a wrinkled old man on a bus who leaned across the aisle and offered me the equivalent of $1.50 for my wedding ring. As the lifting of his shirt exposed a longer and longer blade, I took his offer more and more seriously.

So sharp objects were on my mind as I hopped off the Karakorum Highway and onto the doorstep of the cheapest hotel in Tashkurgan. On a fixed grad student budget, this was no time to splurge, and I opted for a dirt-cheap dormitory with four beds to a room. Let my Chinese roommates gawk and stare at my chest hair, genetic insecurities be damned. At least I would have enough money for lunch.

But the imagined Chinese roommates turned out to be Pakistanis, decked out in white robes, traditional layered headgear, and everything else I remembered from sensational reports on CNN.

This was the summer of 2007, after all. The war in Iraq had no end in sight. As an American who had grown up in the whitest suburbs of the whitest part of the country, Seattle, I had never met a Muslim in my life, much less shared a room with one.

Any insecurities I may have had about my chest hair soon vanished. One look at their bushy beards and forearms told me these guys were far more hirsute than I. Not only that, but they had the biggest knives I had ever seen in my life—blades that would put any Uyghur man to shame.

Suddenly nervous, I laid my backpack on the one vacant bed, and in the silence, a single question came to mind: Who slaughters a sheep with a machete?

All three Pakistanis were staring at me, in open defiance of the American Stare Rule: when your gaze has been detected, you must look away.

They don't look away.

One of the older men stands up. In his hand is a blade that I can only describe as a cutlass. He steps toward me. His face seems fixed in grim determination. In an instant, my years of carefully cultivated postcolonial sympathy for the downtrodden peoples of the world vanish into thin, Foucauldian air. Standing by my bed, I'm frozen.

Images of a breaking-news banner headline flashed into my mind. Tomorrow's *Fox News* lead: "American Grad Student Killed in Western China; Mom Urged Him Not to Go."

Three steps away.

Two.

Face to face.

He bends down. A sharp glint somewhere below my waist. Scenes of disembowelment flash through my mind.

I look down, expecting to see my innards splashed about on the ground.

Instead, he holds a watermelon, cut into shimmering quarters.

"Please," the man says, in perfect English, "eat with us."

MAINLANDER

Jeremy A. Murray

2008

In the late summer of 2008, while living on China's southern island of Hainan, I compulsively followed the distant American news cycle.

Even on my snail-paced Internet connection, I tried to stay abreast of every twist and turn in the final weeks of the Obama-McCain presidential race. I would wait hours while my laptop connection buffered the latest episode of *Meet the Press*.

Like many Americans, I was exhausted by eight years of bungling imperial leadership, and I was eager to see a new administration begin repairing the damage. During the final weeks of the second Bush's second term, the long days dragged heavily in the Hainan heat. The humidity was relentless, and nights were sometimes too hot for sleep until a friend suggested a trick: soak a towel, wring out as much water as possible, then lay it flat over the mattress and sleep on it for a cooling effect. In the morning, the towel and mattress were dry, and even on the hottest nights you could get some sleep. Now it was just the fate of the Union keeping me awake.

I lived on the campus of Hainan University (Haida) in the island's provincial capital of Haikou, on its north coast. I was conducting doctoral research on the Communist revolutionary movement there. While my research kept me busy, I was always eager to talk about American politics with friends, always primed to relate my frustrations, anxieties, and hopes. Then, in October, with the election only days away, I was invited by the university's Communist Youth League to give a talk about American history and Sino-U.S. relations.

The students in the youth league were a bright and thoughtful group from all around China. They were cheerful and even seemed enthusiastic to hear the talk. I had planned a sober discussion of opium, Anson Burlingame, the Open Door, Hu Shih, Joseph Stilwell, Zhou Enlai, and the possibility of a new special relationship; but my overheated and agitated state on the eve of the American election led me somehow to shift gears into a raving jeremiad on the dangerous and myopic foreign policy of the outgoing American administration. I ended with some choice and frothy words about the president's officious and obnoxious religiosity, and his Christian moralizing and righteousness, which was typical, I felt, of American exceptionalism. I didn't hold back, and the stunned faces in the audience made me quickly feel I'd overstepped.

A polite reception followed, but the room was mostly quiet. With generous smiles and nods, everyone filed out. I knew one of the students as a neighbor, and we walked back toward the dorms together, mostly in silence. I finally asked him if he thought I was out of line. "Well, I guess maybe we felt a little awkward. But I enjoyed it . . . and

I agreed with most of it. Except for the end, to be honest. My Mom is a Christian and prays every day. From the way you spoke, I think maybe you don't know enough Christians."

In the Hainan summer and well into the autumn, the hot nights are lively and boisterous with night markets, sports, and other communal fun. Since most Hainanese take a long midday nap to get them through the hottest hours of the day, they don't finally turn in until very late in the evening. The custom makes perfect sense, but many mainlanders consider it to be a mark of the characteristic indolence of the "backward" islanders. I eventually adopted the schedule myself. After finishing an afternoon-evening session in the library, I would venture out for a late dinner and some exercise at 8 or 9 at night.

The hardest-hitting volleyball matches I've ever seen began after sundown on the campus's sand courts under orange floodlights. The best players were all ringers—local guys who weren't students. They showed up to take over the courts as soon as they got off work, with cigarettes in their mouths and two or three tall beer bottles in each hand. Most of the students who had been playfully patting a ball back and forth didn't need to be asked to move on when the ringers arrived. It only took a few spikes, delivered with a shout of "*WO SHAAA!*" (*I KILL . . . !*), to make most of the daunted Haida students head for the basketball courts.

After about a week of trying to join, I was normalized into the games, but only after running a gauntlet of target practice: *WO SHA!* bump, set, *WO SHA!* bump, set, *WO SHA!* bump, set, *WO SHA!* . . . In those first few games, I suspected that some of our side's blockers neglected their duties and intentionally allowed a few spikes to come whistling through just to see the *laowai* (foreigner) get a bloody nose. Either way, I had to play a few games with wads of reddened toilet paper in both nostrils. The ringers were mostly tall and wiry. Fishermen, cooks, construction workers, cab drivers—when they leapt, their feet left the sand and they seemed to hover for a leisurely moment as they aimed and hammered home a perfect kill: *WO SHA!* . . . Then they floated down to survey the damage.

Beers and smokes between the games were friendly, but the chatter was mostly in Hainanese, and I understood only a few words. Eventually, someone might welcome me into the conversation in Mandarin. In spite of my enjoyment of the game and the company, my one-track obsession with American politics would still inexorably turn the talk from their jokes in Hainanese to some glum pap about Bush, McCain, and Obama, conveyed in my wooden Mandarin. The conversation would sputter, and clunk, and then stop altogether. I was a downer.

After a glum moment or two, a few eye rolls, and a rallying hand clap, it was a relief for everyone to return to the game and high spirits. "Hey, man, you talk like a mainlander!" somebody offered from across the net. I think he meant both my stiff accent and my sober conversation. "Study our Hainan island and you'll learn to relax!"

悟

AVOIDING LONG LINES

Paul G. Pickowicz

2010

In spring 2010, I was teaching a course on silent-era Chinese cinema of the 1920s and 1930s at East China Normal University in Shanghai. I had more than forty students, half undergraduates and half graduate students. The school set me up in a very comfortable apartment on the grounds of its spiffy new campus in the Minhang suburb. The new campus was glittering, but a bit nondescript. It would not have been out of place in Iowa or South Dakota—except, of course, for the uniformed security guards who policed every entrance. On weekends, it was very quiet on campus, a bit too quiet. On occasion, I was bored. The students seemed bored every weekend. Once in a while, a few students and I would take the shuttle bus into the city and spend pleasant hours strolling around the old French Concession, looking for surviving art deco buildings of the 1920s, talking about architecture, looking for the hidden-away former residences of people like Mao's wife Jiang Qing, and searching out funky coffee shops.

The grand Shanghai World Expo opened while I was there. Every time I met my class, the students asked, "Have you been to the Expo yet?"

I responded the same way each time: "Sorry. It's not my kind of thing. I can't stand crowds like that, and I positively hate to stand in long lines—for anything." The press was reporting waits of two to three hours for some of the most popular pavilions, including the

Japanese exhibition. To make matters worse, as the Expo progressed, the weather became hotter and hotter.

"Have you been to the Expo yet?" they repeated.

"Long lines, too hot, no way," I repeated. Worried about terrorist attacks and bad publicity of any sort, the police conducted airport-type security checks at the entrance to all Shanghai subway stops and prohibited the sale of knives, meat cleavers, and rat poison.

But some of the students wouldn't take no for an answer. One of them showed up in class with a free Expo ticket for me. "Very clever. How could I say no?" I thought. I agreed to go, but I protested again about long lines.

"I won't stand there like a fool in a two-hour line. I don't care how good the exhibits are." But the students, a few closet wise guys among them, were several steps ahead of me.

"We've thought of that already. We have a plan that will be very interesting, but avoid long lines. Trust us!"

Eager to know more about this ingenious plan, I asked for the details.

"We've done a bit of research. Instead of going to the *most* popular pavilions, we will visit the *least* popular. There will be no lines and we can try our best to figure out why these places are so unpopular." I couldn't resist quizzing them about what their research had shown.

"Which is the most unpopular pavilion?" I asked.

"That's easy," they responded. "North Korea. We'll visit that one first!" This was very mischievous, but I had to admit that they had my full attention now, and I was looking forward to the trip.

Upon arrival at the sprawling and jam-packed Expo, we headed immediately to the North Korea pavilion. Would the students be able to keep a straight face? Would I be able to keep a straight face? Walking over to the North Korea pavilion, we passed the Japan pavilion. I went to the end of the line and asked the last person standing how much time it would take to get in.

"Probably two and a half hours," he said smiling.

Finally we reached the North Korea pavilion. It was small and featured bare-bones construction. There was no one in line, not even one person. The one-room interior was sparse: a small, artificial tea garden, some large propaganda photos, a bank of TV monitors showing propaganda documentaries, and a couple of counters selling souvenirs. The space was practically empty, except for four or five Korean staff members, all of whom spoke very good Chinese. There was nothing to do, so I thought the visit would last only a few minutes and we would be on our way to the next no-line stop.

But then I noticed that among the souvenirs being sold were North Korea postage stamps. As an avid collector of Asian stamps, I was instantly attracted to the display. I spoke at great length in Chinese to the middle-aged Korean man behind the counter. I gave him my card and he gave me his.

"You're American!" he said.

"I'm an American stamp collector!" I responded. I added that this was the very first pavilion of my visit to the Expo. Slowly but surely, a crowd began to gather, everyone eager to hear what we were saying. I ended up buying one of everything in order to launch my North Korean collection. The bill was over 900 *yuan*, no doubt the largest sale of the day, perhaps their largest of the Expo. At one point, I looked up at the crowd and noticed a fancy video camera filming the spectacle.

"Who is that?" I wondered.

As I walked away, the cameraman came over to me. He said he was from Shanghai TV and asked if he could interview me on camera.

"Sure, why not?" I said. He thought the whole thing was a curious human-interest story and wanted to work out a good script.

"I'll ask you why you're in Shanghai, and you say you're a visiting American professor at East China Normal. Then I'll ask you why you chose to visit the North Korea pavilion first. Then, after you answer that, please hold up the stamp packets so everyone can see." My students could barely contain themselves. With the camera rolling, we finally got to the part about why I chose North Korea first. I didn't have the heart to tell the truth. I wanted to blame the students for the awkward situation I was in. Instead, I simply said that since the USA and North Korea have no diplomatic relations, this was a rare opportunity for me to meet some North Koreans and have a friendly chat—people-to-people diplomacy. When I discovered the stamps, I explained, it made the friendly back-and-forth chat very easy and very pleasant. The cameraman was delighted with this charming story.

Outside, I chided my unruly students.

"Look at the trouble you guys got me into!" I quipped.

"Come on, hurry up," they responded. "Laos is over here!"

悟

HAINAN FISHING CAPTAIN

Jeremy A. Murray

2012

Under a blue tarp strung between palm trees on a white beach, in the heat of a Hainan summer afternoon, we got drunk. My wife and I were the feasted guests of some new acquaintances, a group that included energetic retirees from Beijing and some local fishermen. Our hosts had invited us to the secluded and hastily assembled restaurant for a late lunch. To reassure us that the food was good in spite of the place's ramshackle appearance, one of our hosts told us it was a favorite hideaway for big officials and their "*xiaosan*," or mistresses (literally "little number threes").

I was new to this part of Hainan, and grateful for the welcoming gesture. The food really was exceptional, and the beer was refreshing and our glasses never empty. The conversation, which was uproarious, was mainly about amusing differences between China and America and included plenty of jokes about the insatiable appetites and unaccountable excesses of the place's bigwig clientele.

Eventually, the beer and the sun took their toll on all of us, and the talk mellowed and slowed. I was more than ready for the customary afternoon nap. But then one of our Beijing hosts seemed to regain his focus and seriousness. He squinted at me: "You study Hainan's heroes, right? You know he's one?" He jutted his chin toward a quiet companion who sat a bit apart from the group. The man, lean and darkly tanned, wore a goatee and was smoking a maroon-colored cigarette. His legs were crossed, he was dressed neatly, and he seemed comfortable in the heat. He acknowledged his friend from Beijing with a thin smile. My host went on, "He's a fishing captain, detained in the Philippines. Three months." My Beijing host leaned back to gauge my reaction. He crossed his legs, perhaps in a study of the captain.

I had been following the news of flare-ups among the several countries that claimed territory in the South China Sea. Even as we were enjoying that lunch in the summer of 2012, the issue of disputed maritime and island claims had reignited anti-Japanese sentiment in China. Violent nationalist demonstrations were breaking out around the country related to a series of arrests, detentions, and diplomatic incidents around the Diaoyutai (or Senkaku) Islands. American destroyers plowed through on their "freedom of navigation operations." I knew enough to keep my research work safely distant from this kind of topic because mention of it could complicate my access at the Hainan archives. My focus stayed on the early twentieth century.

Our host from Beijing turned expectantly to the captain, clearly hoping for some kind of speech for the foreign guests. The captain did not oblige.

"When did it happen?" prodded our host. The captain replied in a few dry words, reluctant to be the center of attention.

But I was beginning to share our host's interest and blurted, "Was it great hardship?" I remember his look of sober patience, and another thin smile.

"Well, the jailers were really nice guys," began the captain. Our Beijing host scowled and started to speak, but the captain turned to him and continued, "But we weren't allowed any alcohol for three months, and . . . ," he held up his elegant cigarette, " . . . the cigarettes they gave us were lousy." The table erupted once more in laughter and our Beijing host stood up, mopped his brow, and proposed a toast to the captain.

BLACK IS BEAUTIFUL!

Marketus D. Presswood

2013

In 2013, I worked in Beijing as a program director for an American study-abroad program. One of my many responsibilities was to plan a weeklong trip to either Yunnan or Qinghai province. My American students would get a chance to experience life in one of the more rustic parts of China and to travel in areas where many minority groups lived. It was going to be a great reprieve from the crowds of über-urban Beijing. Given the time of the year, I opted for Qinghai, a western province on the Tibetan Plateau with a large Tibetan population. The weather would be pleasantly comfortable in September—cool and mild. The itinerary included a trip to Qinghai's Sangke Grasslands.

We arrived in the afternoon and had a quick picnic-type lunch with sundry snacks that included peanut-butter-and-jelly sandwiches. The sky was deep blue except for some puffy white clouds, and the grass seemed as if it stretched past the horizon. Our first activity was horseback riding. We met our Tibetan guides, who gave us quick pointers about riding, and we hopped on various kinds of horses. All of our Tibetan guides, who rode alongside us to ensure our horses stayed the course, appeared to be around our age, but their leathery faces were a bit weather-worn from exposure to the elements. The color of their faces ranged from a tannish brown to a bronzed copper that gleamed in the light, giving them a regal and elegant look despite deep wrinkles.

We were not the only tourists on the grasslands that day. While horseback riding, we passed some Han Chinese tourists headed in the opposite direction. One of them, looking in my direction, yelled in Mandarin, *"Ta name hei!"* (He's so black!)

I quipped in response, *"Hei shi mei de!"* (Black is beautiful!) The Tibetans in my group and those accompanying the Han tourist group, most of whose skin was as dark as mine, or darker, erupted in triumphant laughter at my repartee. The comeback not only rhymed in Chinese but expressed pride in the beauty and dignity of minority ethnic identity—in both their case and mine. It seemed as if they had seldom heard or dared utter anything so demonstrative and public in response to the Han majority, who, no doubt, frequently derided their "too-dark" skin color.

All that day and the next, I heard the Tibetans laughing and smiling as they spoke in Tibetan while pointing at me. I could understand only the Mandarin *"hei shi mei de"* as it went by. But it was clear what was happening. The Tibetans who heard the story beamed with pride and joy. James Brown would be proud.

悟

DARTH VADER AND THE TRICERATOPS

Maggie Greene

2014

In 2010 and 2011, I lived in Shanghai doing research for my dissertation on Chinese opera during the Mao years. I spent countless hours looking for materials—operas, plays, whole runs of journals, even things stamped "materials for criticism"—that I found on a secondhand-book site called kongfz.com. I also began collecting "fun" ephemera, in part to learn how my formal research topic was fitting into the broader context of what ordinary people found interesting. *Lianhuanhua* (linked picture books), which are something like American comic books, drew my attention. I went looking for them, especially for ones from the 1950s and 1960s that told supernatural tales.

They were inexpensive, only about one U.S. dollar apiece (unless they were of Cultural Revolution vintage, because those had become collector's items and therefore cost much more). Purchasing online was fine, but I found it even more fun to browse physically, and I did this by going about once a month to the Wen Miao book fair at the Confucian temple in Shanghai. It had everything. One paid a small entrance fee, and then the sky was the limit.

I have a vivid memory of one particular rickety table that featured *lianhuanhua*. There were heaps of them—literally *heaps*—on the table, under the table, beside the table. As I approached, the vendor greeted me and asked in halting English what I was looking for. I answered in Chinese that I wanted *lianhuanhua* from the 1950s and 1960s, specifically ones that involved ghosts and spirits. He pulled out some offerings, and I shook my head at most of them. As I was telling him, finally, that I'd take this one and that one, he pulled out one that he said I should take for sure.

I looked at it. It was not ghost opera. It wasn't opera at all, nor was it based on classical literature. It wasn't even from the years of high socialism; the colors were too bright, and the art style was different. I stared at it for a few seconds. It showed a weird tableau washed in bright turquoisey blues, a vaguely pre-Raphaelite-looking woman with long hair and a gun, and . . . a guy with a lightsaber? Eventually I looked at the pinyin title that ran down the left side of the cover: *Xingqiu dazhan.* Star war? . . . Oh, *Star Wars!*

I am not a *Star Wars* fan. I saw the first film and am aware of the whole cultural phenomenon, but that's as far as it goes. I flipped the book over to check the publication data. The state-run press clearly was expecting a lot of interest: *315,000 copies! In 1980?!* Had the *Star Wars* film even hit China by 1980? Surely not, I thought. The Cultural Revolution had barely ended. *And what in the hell does this have to do with your dissertation?* I asked myself. Well, nothing—here it was, the vendor had been friendly, and what was another 8 *yuan*, after all? Pocket change. I bought it.

When I got back to my apartment and took a closer look, I noticed that some of the panels seemed odd. What was a reference to the Kennedy Space Center doing there? Is that . . . Darth Vader? With a *dinosaur*? Why is an extra from *Planet of the Apes* standing in for Chewbacca? It was interesting, but I tossed it temporarily into my pile of ephemera. I had more important fish to fry, like all those serious documents that I needed to get through, the ones written by people whose stories I assumed had "shaped life" in China from 1949 during the Mao years.

Three years later, in May 2014, I was unpacking my last boxes after a move to Bozeman, Montana. There was clothing, kitchenware, and, yes, my collection of books and ephemera. For the first time, I actually sat down and looked at *Star Wars* with some care. Within the first few pages, there were clear references to—even outright copies from—the mid-1970s Japanese anime *Space Battleship Yamato*. There were also toaster ovens, rice cookers, nude statues, J&B whiskey adverts, Russian cosmonauts, and the Kennedy Space Center.

Curious, I started googling. No, *Star Wars* had not been released in the PRC in 1980. Yet here, before my eyes, was a Chinese version of *Star Wars*. The text was boring—but those images! A fascinating pastiche of *all sorts* of globally circulating culture. When? Why? How? Was the PRC *this* global in 1980? Russian cosmonauts I could understand—but 1970s Japanese anime? *Planet of the Apes*?

I snapped a few photos with my iPhone and posted them to Facebook. Several friends—both China scholars and *Star Wars* fans—excitedly asked if I would put up more. "Is that a toaster oven?" they asked. "What's the Kennedy Space Center doing there?" So I scanned the whole book, wrote up a blog post, and linked it on Facebook and Twitter. I thought this would slake the curiosity of a few China hands, and that would be it. Nope. A few days later, I was flooded with hits— *ten thousand* on one day.

And the ball kept rolling. My post, a cleaned-up scan that a friend had produced, and another friend's English translation of the insipid text, started working their way across the Internet. *South China Morning Post. BBC Online. CNN. Rolling Stone.* A Japanese newspaper even tracked down one of the original artists. I began to appear in advertisements for walking tours of the Wen Miao book fair: "One historian found a 1980s *Star Wars* graphic novel from long before the movie ever reached China—who knows what treasures you might unearth here?"

That 1980 *Star Wars* comic might prove to be my longest-lasting— or at least the most highly publicized—contribution to the field of Chinese history. In any case, it made me reevaluate much of what I *thought* I knew about Mao's China, the Cultural Revolution, and life immediately after. Now I had to account for the fact that four years after the end of the Cultural Revolution, an artist working for a state-sponsored press in the PRC had imagined a scene from *Star Wars*—a film officially released in the country more than thirty years later—by adapting a 1970 cover illustration by an American fantasy artist of a sci-fi novel, *A Princess of Mars*, that was first published in 1912. The effort had resulted in an officially published, 315,000-copy run of a palm-sized Chinese book featuring Darth Vader wearing a strappy leather outfit and cape, holding aloft a sword as he kneels on absurdly muscular legs—in front of a triceratops. In China. In 1980.

A PHONE CALL FROM THE PARTY SECRETARY

Melinda Liu

2016

Even as a child, born in Minneapolis, I was accustomed to hearing different Chinese regional dialects. My parents had come from Jiangsu and often spoke the mellifluous Suzhou tongue, but they used the

Shanghai dialect with their many Shanghainese friends. My mother (who was actually born in Beijing) tried to teach my brothers and me standard Mandarin when we were young; we comprehended some simple words, but really didn't speak it.

In the 1970s, I began dabbling with the idea of learning Chinese properly. Very quickly I learned of the deep-rooted bias favoring "pure" Mandarin taught by a native of Beijing.

My obsession with the Beijing dialect kicked into high gear when I landed in Taipei in 1973 to learn Peking (Beijing) opera. I was surrounded by aging teachers, musicians, and other aficionados of that esoteric world, most of them old Beijing natives. It dawned on me that mastering the quirks of their dialect—the tonal clarity, the overly effusive politeness, the curled tongue—could be my ticket toward acceptance.

The Peking opera school where I trained had a cranky hair-and-makeup artist. He was an extremely thin, white-haired man from Beijing who curled his tongue for his *r*'s like crazy; he would drink too much *maotai* liquor and lurch about singing in falsetto to his arrogant white Pekinese (what else?) dog. I can still hear him now, scolding me as he plastered my forehead with gooey hair attachments and my face with white powder before an opera performance.

But when I arrived in Beijing in 1980 to open *Newsweek*'s Beijing bureau, I began to realize my idea of a "pure" Beijing dialect was a fungible notion. Even traveling just an hour by car outside the Chinese capital—still within the boundaries of the Beijing municipality—I encountered rural Chinese who spoke as if they had marbles in their mouths. A Chinese friend told me the retroflexed consonants so typical of northern speech—also called "cacuminal consonants," spoken with the tip of the tongue curled up toward the hard palate—did not easily sound natural when spoken by people who aren't Beijing natives. Translation: Beijing dialect, when spoken by non-Beijingers, can sound like an affectation.

And I threw out my outmoded notions about regional dialects completely after one memorable encounter in 2016. It all started with a phone call. My husband and I happened to be in the valley of the Ming tombs, a rural area where we'd fixed up a cottage not far from the city center and still part of Beijing.

When I picked up my cell phone, the voice on the other end was deep, authoritative, and (at least I thought) pretty standard

Mandarin, though not Beijing dialect. I didn't recognize who it was. He said, "You know who I am, right?"

At the time I'd been trying to upgrade the electricity supply at the cottage, in order to install a heat pump powered by electricity, to connect to the under-floor heating. I'd just talked with the Party secretary of the village—his surname was Ying—about my request a few days earlier. This must be him, I thought. "Are you Party Secretary Ying?" I asked. "Are you calling about that electricity issue?"

The voice chuckled. "You guessed very accurately," he said. He asked if I could come to his office Tuesday "about a certain matter." The "Party secretary" said he needed me to help him give a gift to a visiting government official. He didn't want to present the guy with cash or an expensive material object because of the ongoing anticorruption campaign. This made sense, since the drive to root out corrupt officials was still being pursued ferociously by President Xi Jinping and his right-hand man Wang Qishan, then his anti-graft czar.

The "Party secretary" asked if I could transfer some money into the visiting official's bank account, "and then I'll pay you back when we meet," he said. He texted me a bank account number and a name.

Suspicious, I pointed out that it would be even more incriminating for the official to be receiving money from a foreign citizen. The "Party secretary" insisted it would be okay. I asked him, "If I help you with your problem, will you help me with mine? I need to get the under-floor heating ready before winter." He assured me, "Of course! Just phone me immediately after you make the transfer."

I figured the chances of getting paid back by the "Party secretary" were slim—but it might still be worthwhile if my "help" to him could speed up the process of upgrading the electricity supply. We negotiated for a while over the amount; initially he asked for RMB 10,000, but I said I didn't have that much cash and would need to get it transferred from abroad, which would take days. He said he needed to conduct the transaction right away. We settled on RMB 5,000.

But I was wary, still thinking it was probably a scam. I called a Chinese friend who lived in the village, a well-respected local builder who'd done a lot of work on the cottage. I explained what had happened and asked, "Do you think it's really our Party secretary? Would he ask for a favor like that?" Tellingly, the builder answered, "I have no idea, but it likely is him." I gave the builder the phone number and he called it; no one answered.

Tuesday came; I was still worried the guy on the phone was a fraud. My husband and I discussed whether we should ask to meet the "Party secretary" in person after the transfer. I didn't think that would prove anything; if he were a criminal he'd simply agree to meet us, then not show up. I dawdled, a thick stack of *renminbi* burning a hole in my pocket.

Just at that moment, a neighbor appeared at our cottage. He lived close by, was handy with tools and plants, and kept an eye on the cottage when we weren't there. And his surname was Ying. It dawned on me that I should ask him about "Party Secretary Ying": "He's your relative, right? Do you know him well? Is he honest? Will he help us with the electricity upgrade?"

I explained my suspicions about the caller. Neighbor Ying thought a moment, then said, "If you give him the money, he won't necessarily be able to help with the electricity." We hit on a plan. I would phone "Party Secretary Ying" on my cell phone, then put him on speakerphone. My neighbor would listen to the call to determine if it was his relative or not.

I phoned the "Party secretary." The guy clearly thought he was close to closing the transaction. In previous conversations, he'd spoken sparingly, taking care not to mention details. Now, the voice on the other end of the line was ebullient and loquacious. I kept him chatting on the line. My neighbor listened intently—then silently shook his head no.

My neighbor suddenly blurted out to the guy on the phone: "Who are you?" The voice replied, "I'm Ying, the Party secretary." My neighbor shouted gruffly, "No! You're not the Party secretary! He's my 'brother' and you're not him. You don't even speak like him. You're a fraud from southern China!" The voice fell silent. CLICK. The line went dead.

Neighbor Ying said, "Couldn't you tell he's not from this village? He doesn't talk like us. He's from Zhejiang, or maybe Shanghai. Do you know how to tell southerners when they speak?" He explained they might say *suji,* instead of *shuji,* for "Party secretary" in *putonghua*—and some Zhejiang natives "have such strange accents there's no way to understand them."

My learning curve had come full circle. Here I was getting a lesson on cacuminal consonants and lingua-alveolar fricatives from an elderly Chinese farmer, probably about the same age as the gruff Peking opera makeup man who'd scolded me more than four decades earlier in Taipei. Previously I thought my neighbor often talked as if his mouth was full of stones. But at this moment, having just heard him tell off the fake "Party secretary," I resolved never again to complain when I couldn't understand him.

Afterword

Minxin Pei

The trips of this group of Westerners—mainly scholars of China during their formative years of professional training—collectively constitute a journey of discovery, cultural engagement, and political learning. Years, if not decades, have passed since their trips ended, but this metaphorical journey continues. Despite their varying professional accomplishments, all of the authors are continuing their quest of trying to understand China and, in the process, understand themselves and their own countries and cultures.

In the meantime, China's own journey—away from poverty, isolation, and repression—remains unfinished. To be sure, the country has made tremendous progress since our colleagues first visited. Indeed, few of them could have imagined the economic progress and social transformation China has achieved in the last four decades. Yet, economically, China still has a long way to go before reaching the status of a high-income society. Politically, the prospect of establishing a liberal democracy and the rule of law in a country governed for millennia by despotic regimes and ravaged by the rule of man is still a distant dream.

The anecdotes told by the authors featured in this volume are not meant simply to entertain, although they do so, each in their unique ways. Their stories have important educational value as well. Together they reveal a China that has, thanks to the progress in the post-Mao era, disappeared or receded from our collective memory. Indeed, few visitors to China today, including budding scholars, will encounter the same conditions experienced by those who dared to venture into the Middle Kingdom during and immediately after the madness of the Cultural Revolution and more than two decades of self-imposed isolation. Nevertheless, reading these stories can usefully remind us of the scars of China's political turmoil, the human indignity of grinding poverty, and the comic tragedy of cultural isolation.

Perhaps the most revealing aspect of these stories capturing the authors' "Aha!" moments is the cultural gap between China and the West that was created by ignorance, innocent but erroneous assumptions, and lack of contact between China and the outside world during the Mao era. Western scholars went to China during and immediately after the Cultural Revolution with a limited understanding of subtle Chinese cultural norms and practices. Many of them did not appreciate deeply enough the psychological trauma, cultural destruction, and economic deprivation inflicted by Mao's rule on Chinese society. Yet, as individuals who knew a lot more about China than average Westerners, our colleagues had ostensibly reasonable assumptions about China and operated on them. What is revealed by these various "Aha!" moments is the error of these assumptions more than anything else, and the lessons quickly learned as a result. The authors' candor is striking and makes the collection valuable and indeed unique. Through the decades, the vignettes in this collection vary, but this theme of candid recollections, of stumbling and learning, continues.

China studies has come a long way, thanks in large part to early visitors to the People's Republic, who not only opened lines of cultural and intellectual contact, but also educated the ensuing generations of China scholars. We now have a much better understanding of China. China has also changed, and its people now know more about Westerners and their cultural quirks as well. Indeed, a companion or sequel volume could feature anecdotes and vignettes by scholars who were born in China and traveled to the United States or other Western countries, narrating the profound transformations of past decades from that vantage. These metaphorical journeys—both our individual journeys as scholars in search of knowledge, and China's journey in search of prosperity and human dignity—are in the right direction even though they are still in progress.

About the Contributors

Nick Admussen is Assistant Professor of Chinese Literature and Culture at Cornell University.

Jennifer Anderson is a doctoral graduate from the Creative Writing and China Studies programs at Monash University in Melbourne, Australia.

Jeremy Brown is Associate Professor of History at Simon Fraser University.

Suzanne Cahill is Adjunct Professor Emerita at the University of California, San Diego.

Anita Chan is co-editor of *The China Journal* and Visiting Fellow of the Department of Political and Social Change, Australian National University.

Donald Clarke is Professor of Law and David Weaver Research Professor of Law at the George Washington University Law School.

James A. Cook is Associate Director of the Asian Studies Center at the University of Pittsburgh.

Joseph W. Esherick is Distinguished Professor Emeritus of History at the University of California, San Diego.

Charlotte Furth is Professor Emerita of Chinese History at the University of Southern California.

Dru C. Gladney is Professor of Anthropology at Pomona College, in Claremont, California.

Thomas D. Gorman retired as Chairman and Editor-in-Chief of *Fortune* China in 2016.

Maggie Greene is Assistant Professor of History at Montana State University, Bozeman.

James M. Hargett is Professor of Chinese at the University at Albany, State University of New York.

Justin M. Jacobs is Associate Professor of History at American University.

Wendy Larson is Professor Emerita at the University of Oregon, Eugene.

Perry Link is Chancellorial Chair for Teaching Across Disciplines at the University of California, Riverside.

Melinda Liu is an award-winning foreign correspondent and *Newsweek* Beijing Bureau Chief.

Stephen R. MacKinnon is Professor Emeritus of History at Arizona State University.

Richard P. Madsen is Distinguished Professor Emeritus of Sociology at the University of California, San Diego.

Andrew D. Morris is Professor of History at California Polytechnic State University, San Luis Obispo.

David Moser is Associate Dean at the Yenching Academy of Peking University.

Jeremy A. Murray is Associate Professor of History at California State University, San Bernardino.

Minxin Pei is the Tom and Margot Pritzker '72 Professor of Government and George R. Roberts Fellow at Claremont McKenna College.

Paul G. Pickowicz is Distinguished Professor Emeritus of History and Chinese Studies at the University of California, San Diego.

Marketus D. Presswood is a doctoral candidate in Modern Chinese History at the University of California, Irvine.

Stanley Rosen is Professor of Political Science at the University of Southern California.

Morris Rossabi is Distinguished Professor of History at the City University of New York and Adjunct Professor of History at Columbia University.

Vera Schwarcz was the Freeman Professor of History and East Asian Studies at Wesleyan University for four decades and is currently Research Associate at the Hebrew University in Jerusalem.

Jeffrey N. Wasserstrom is Chancellor's Professor of History at the University of California, Irvine.

Martin King Whyte is John Zwaanstra Professor Emeritus of International Studies and Sociology at Harvard University.

Philip F. Williams is Professor Emeritus of Chinese at Arizona State University and Teaching Professor of Chinese at Montana State University.

Mayfair Mei-hui Yang is Professor of Religious Studies and East Asian Languages & Cultural Studies at the University of California, Santa Barbara.

Geoffrey Ziebart retired in 2016 as President, China, for Crane Company.

Printed in Great
Britain
by Amazon